My Parents Got Old!
Now What Do I Do?

My Parents Got Old!
Now What Do I Do?

A Practical Guide to Caring for Your Aging Parents

JANINE BROWN

ARCHWAY PUBLISHING

Archway Publishing books may be ordered through booksellers or by contacting:

Archway Publishing
1663 Liberty Drive
Bloomington, IN 47403
www.archwaypublishing.com
1 (888) 242-5904

ISBN: 978-1-4808-2297-9 (sc)
ISBN: 978-1-4808-2298-6 (e)

Library of Congress Control Number: 2015916263

Print information available on the last page.

Archway Publishing rev. date: 11/6/2015

This book is dedicated to my two sisters, who paved the way for me to learn as much as I could regarding caring for parents.

CONTENTS

ACKNOWLEDGMENTS

I would like to acknowledge several groups of people, including the Writer's Group, who helped marshal this book to fruition. Also, I would like to thank so many friends and colleagues who encouraged me to write this book, and the Alzheimer's and dementia organizations for allowing me to volunteer at their health fairs.

INTRODUCTION

I've been a caregiver. I learned a lot, and I want to share it. There is no sense in you struggling to learn what I already know. That would be silly. When we as a family went through this, I talked with a lot of people who were facing similar circumstances. None of us knew a lot, but everyone knew a little bit. Leverage existing knowledge. It'll save you time, money, and stress—I promise.

This book is geared to those who are caregivers for an elderly person. The references, examples, and perspectives are all about caring for a parent. However, I realize that not all caregiving is for a parent. So though I use the word *parent* in this book, the advice applies to whomever you are supporting, but it is not for those of you caregiving for a young person.

I've included real examples but have changed the parameters of the incidents to protect the privacy of the individuals.

After my father died, I took a while to process all that had happened. It had happened over several years. I began to think that caregiving for an elderly parent was a project. Being a project manager, that insight clarified for me how to approach the issue. For me, it gave a structured process to handle these difficult issues. My sisters were the heavy-lifters for my parents. My husband and I were the caregivers for his parents.

All projects have beginnings, ends, and constraints. Constraints include time, money, geography, resources, data, and information. Projects have critical paths, unexpected happenings, contingencies, drama, resolutions, and stress. And someone needs to manage it. Maybe it's you, maybe it's another sibling, or maybe you hire someone to manage it. You are one of the resources for this project, so the more you know, the more you can help or support.

In each chapter, I discuss the details of the topic not from a professional perspective (like a doctor or lawyer) but from a caregiver perspective. That perspective is different. I discuss the costs, time, and money. I also guide you to available resources. I give examples of things that have happened—and all examples are *real*. I helped a few people with the issues mentioned within this book as they were going through them. This book is a compilation of what I learned from dealing with those issues, the approaches I used, and the knowledge needed.

In chapters 2, 4, and 5, I lay out the essential items for you to know about health care for parents and the legal and financial concerns. This doesn't mean you have to become a health care professional or a lawyer, but you do need to know some stuff. A lot of the crises caregivers face stem from the health area, and a lot of unnecessary problems come from the legal and financial realms.

Chapter 3 is about the daily life of your parents. It covers quite a few topics about this other area from which crises emanate. By the end of your caregiving, you will know so much about your parents, so much that you never thought about or dreamed you would know. Some of it, you may not want to know. This chapter walks you through your parents' lives and what you need to notice so you can intervene when necessary.

Chapter 6 is about dementia. I talk about the feelings that come with it, offer some helpful hints, and describe what you can and cannot do for someone with dementia. My mother had dementia, and so did my mother-in-law. I also volunteered for an Alzheimer's organization. I learned a lot about what the disease is, how you handle it, and what it means to a family. I also talked to a lot of people faced with this aspect of caregiving as I worked at health fairs.

In chapter 7, I talk about how you keep on track and focused, and chapter 8 is on planning. I try in this chapter to help you put all of it together.

Chapter 9 is about the end, what you need to prepare for and what happens. There's more work here than you may anticipate.

We also discuss what happens if you *do not* do something. In all cases, you choose what you can or cannot do based on the facts and resources you have at the time. Most of this stuff just is—and you need to deal with what is.

If you are still deciding whether you want to buy this book, turn to page xiv. It's a beginning checklist of things that you have to have and know, at a minimum, to be the caregiver resource. If you have all those things covered, you may not need this book, because you're already organized and informed. If not, this book will definitely help you.

Interspersed between chapters are essays, musings, and venting. These sections are about the emotions that occur during this process. At the end of the chapters, there are pages for you to write down what is pertinent for you. It may be what you have to figure out, information you need, or names and numbers of people you might have to contact. Use the notes pages at the end of chapters to keep track of what you need to find out, what you know, or what you need to do or to vent.

If this is the start of your caregiving duties, don't be overwhelmed. While there is a lot to learn and adjust to, there is time. If you have had your first crisis and are lost, this book will help you focus and get organized. The more knowledge you have, the better resource you will be to your parents and to your family. Good luck! And you will survive.

Checklist

Topic	Description	Location/Names/Amounts/Timings
Legal	will	location
	durable power of attorney	names
	health care power of attorney	names/what they want done
	safety deposit box	Where's the key?
	trust document	
	name / address of lawyer	
	in-home safe	contents/combination
	funeral arrangements	payment, location, name of contact
	cemetery plot—location	
Financial	bank name and account numbers	account access, online IDs and passwords
	financial planner name / location / phone	all computer IDs and passwords
	brokerage accounts (name/ number)	
	IRAs, annuities	
	pension names (money and timing)	annuity type
	other income sources	
	life insurance (value/names)	type of life insurance
	bonds (government and other)	
	Social Security	
	veteran's benefits	
	house titles / mortgage / value	
Health	doctors' names / locations	gerontologist, meet doctors
	HIPAA form	or medical authorization document
	drugs used and cost	

Topic	Description	Location/Names/Amounts/Timings
	memory issues	
	have doctor phone numbers on fridge	create a document for emergency help
	in-home help	
	hospital used	
Social	friends/activities/timing	online accounts—like Facebook and other social media
	travel plans	
	driving status / car condition	
	church affiliation / name of pastor	
	names / numbers of neighbors	
	house condition—help?	
Nutrition	weight	Who does the cooking?
	diet	What's in the fridge?
	hydration	
Family Members	primary caregiver	
	phones / cells / e-mails / help list	
	spokesperson	

CHAPTER 1
The Beginning

As Glinda, the good witch of the North from *The Wizard of Oz*, states, "It is always best to start at the beginning."

So now is the beginning. You have started caregiving. You may be surprised to recognize that your parents have aged. I hope they are in relatively good shape, but now you are asking yourself a few questions: What do I do now? Is there anything I can do? How do I go about this?

You have to find out what needs to be done for your parents and either do it or coordinate it. This has nothing to do with how good or bad your relationship with your parents is. It's about responsibility. You have legs. (Maybe their legs aren't so good anymore). This book can help you find out what you need to do with them.

You do not have to do it all. Some natural caregivers think that they need to do it all or begin to believe that. These people are not good delegators, and caregivers *need* to delegate; it's too much to do and handle by yourself. There is plenty of help available. What you need to decide is when you need help, how much help you need, and what you can afford in money, time, and involvement for this feat. If you are not the major caregiver in your family, one of your jobs is to keep the major caregiver going. Support, chip in, volunteer, document information, or do the taxes—and *call*.

Definitions

Caregiving (my definition) is any assistance, direction, and facilitation in support of your elderly parents. For example, you may hire a home-helper to assist your parent in getting up in the morning. You may be working and unable to take time off every morning. So you coordinate the hiring of someone to help.

The *major caregiver* is the spokesperson for the elderly parents and the first in line to be called when crises hit. He or she is the one who makes the decisions and co-ordinates the effort. (Tasks can be delegated). The major caregiver is a dictator. He or she is responsible for informing other caregivers what is needed and what the status is. The major caregiver will seek out opinions about what needs to be done but has the final say-so.

The term *afford* refers to the amount of money, time, and involvement you can spend.

Caregiving is a continuum (see graph 1). Graph 1 is merely an illustration of in-tensity. Yes, it has a beginning and an end, and it has highs and lows. Eventually it ends—but not necessarily when you think it will. That's for the last chapter. For now, we're looking at the beginning.

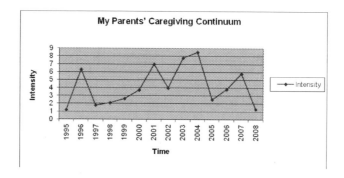

The caregiving continuum can be a multiyear project, and the intensity builds with each new crisis. When a crisis is relieved or resolved, the intensity decreases slightly, but it never goes back to its original level while the person lives.

Caregiving doesn't end when the individual dies. Surprise! Caregiving continues until all issues are dealt with relative to the individual who has died.

Our caregiving duties began in 1999. My sister started it by holding a sibling meeting. We sat down and discussed what we were willing and able to do. And we were honest. The willingness was there but not much knowledge—not then. We knew so little, but we learned.

Conducting a sibling meeting is a good first step in establishing the lines of communication needed for this journey. It can get issues out before they become insurmountable during a crisis and can help get your family organized. The meeting doesn't have to be in person; it can be over the phone or the Internet. And there can be more than one. You don't have to cover everything in one sitting. Holidays sometimes provide an opportunity to sit down together.

We spent thirteen years caregiving. You learn a few things when it's extended that long. As you embed yourself more and more into your parents' lives, your involvement becomes a full-time job. This fact may sneak up on you, and one day, you'll realize you aren't doing the things you used to do. I cancelled many get-togethers with friends. Eventually I stopped accepting or planning to meet up with them. I had no choice. That was just how it worked out. You will find yourself talking about your caregiving activities to everyone (who listens). As a friend told me, I became boring. She said it with caring. I hadn't realized how singular my life had become. Nor will you (more about this in a later chapter).

So how do you start? Caregiving requires knowledge—knowledge of your parents' current lives and their medical, financial, and daily activities.

First, write down (and I do mean write) everything you know about their lives in these three categories:

1. health
2. finances / legal matters
3. daily living

This can be part of your sibling meeting, or you can do it before the meeting. Get a three-ring binder in which to store all your knowledge, or put it online so it's shareable between all siblings.

For example, when it comes to financial knowledge, maybe one of you has done their taxes. If so, you have wonderful knowledge about your parents' finances. Share it. Go through each chapter in this book to get other ideas.

Here's a proposed agenda for the sibling meeting:

1. Objectives of Meeting
   a. Understand what each of you knows about your parents.
   b. Identify what each of you is able to do.
   c. Identify what you don't know about your parents.
   d. Identify what you cannot do, won't do, or don't want to do.
2. Guiding Principles of the Meeting
   a. No judgments.
   b. Keep your ego out of this meeting.
      Note: if you don't, subsequent caregiving will remove all ego from your personality.
   c. All information is good.
   d. This isn't about power, control, or ego.
   e. Be honest with yourself and your siblings. For example, if you really don't want your parents to move in with you, say so. It's not wrong.
3. List of Items
   a. List the items you know about, using the checklist as a starting point.
   b. For unknown items, assign checklist items to individuals.
   c. Decide how to document and communicate new information and who is responsible for it.
4. Priorities
   a. What's a critical item?
   b. If there are no critical items, make the list from top to bottom.
      i. Note: health care power of attorney and HIPAA forms are the most critical.
      ii. The general financial situation needs to be defined.

5. Communications Setup
   a. How will you communicate?
   b. When? How much? Revise this over time.
6. Major Caregiver Role Assignment

Make sure you document the sibling meeting. You wouldn't want anyone to forget what was talked about and decided. At first, you won't remember most of the information, but after a while, it will become second nature. It is a good practice to document all meetings, including meetings with doctors, insurance representatives, and those dealing with financial matters. I talk more about this in the specific chapters dedicated to the individual topic.

Be honest with yourself and your siblings—truly honest. This isn't about your ego or anyone else's. This also isn't about being comfortable. This whole thing is uncomfortable. Try your best. That is what is expected. Sometimes your best may not be good enough. You will learn to accept and live with this.

Remember that this also is not about control. You cannot control what happens. Most of the time, you cannot control your parents either. You can control what you know, however, and knowledge will be enormously helpful to you, your siblings, and your parents.

How do you pick or assign the major caregiver? If you're lucky, your family will have a natural caregiver. It doesn't have to be the oldest, the youngest, the sister, or the doctor in the family. Sometimes one of the siblings volunteers. Sometimes no option is good. You may have no choice but to be the major caregiver. Major caregivers have a burden of responsibility and communication that can be daunting at times. You can ask your siblings who wants to be the major caregiver, but be prepared for the answers.

The major caregiver will

1. be the first person who is called in emergencies;
2. have the ability to drop everything and go see what's going on;
3. communicate with all siblings, relatives, and interested parties;
4. make decisions regarding health, finances, home help, daily living with assistance from the secondary caregivers (this is not done in a vacuum);

5. not necessarily hold the financial or health care powers of attorney (this helps spread out the responsibility and forces communication);
6. keep focused on what is best for the parents;
7. keep and create necessary documentation; and
8. commit to the job of major caregiver.

There are problems in some families when there isn't a natural caregiver or anyone who can handle the job. Then the responsibilities have to be divided and possibly some farmed out to a third party. Maybe there is a neighbor or another relative who might work better. Contact your local aging resource center (these go by many names), and see if they can help you.

Each situation is different and fluid. One may be a major caregiver at first and then be unable to continue. In a family I know, the elderly parents were still mentally acute. The two oldest children held the financial power of attorney and the health care power of attorney. The situation just wasn't working out, so the parents asked another daughter to handle both health and finance matters. This consolidation worked out well for them.

In another family with three children, the eldest sibling—who lived the farthest away—assumed the responsibility. It wasn't perfect, but the eldest was the best out of the three. One sibling was raising a young family, and the closest sibling wasn't always available. The eldest was the only choice. I worked very closely with this individual and outlined very detailed instructions, and the siblings put together a great team to help the mother. They hired a lawyer, a daily money manager, and in-home help, and they set up the powers of attorneys and a trust. It was the best they could do under their circumstances. All of them wanted to be helpful.

Your current situation just may not allow you to be the major caregiver. If you are part of the caregiving team, be considerate of those who aren't yet as accepting as you may be of the situation. Others may react in ways that aren't helpful. And as you work and the other team members work with your particular situation, the ones behind you in acceptance of the situation may handle it better at a later time.

If you can't keep things straight, can't communicate effectively, can't drop everything and go, then you might not be good for the job. Even if you live too far away, you may become a great help (maybe you organize well) to the person left behind. In one family with two siblings, the elderly parent moved in with one of the siblings. The other one, who lived two thousand miles away, worked with that sibling and was kept informed all along the way, even over the distance. The long-distance caregiver started going to the sibling's house for a couple of weeks, then one month, and eventually two months at a time. The long-distance caregiver was able to relieve the other of house issues and caregiving duties. The younger sibling had kids and was still working. Both were great caregivers. In this case, the long-distance sibling did as much as possible, though not everything. Your living situation may not allow you to be the major caregiver. Help where you can, and do what you can.

Sometimes the oldest sibling figures it is his or her job. Maybe you know that he or she won't do a good job because he or she doesn't accept your parents' situation or have the necessary skills to handle the situation. Maybe that sibling doesn't have an adequate understanding or can't be inconvenienced by frantic elderly parents when the parents just started a fire in the home (and not in the fireplace). Maybe you start by volunteering for certain things and thereby begin the major caregiver role. Be prepared to deal with a hurt ego. Keep focused on what the goal is here: to be as much help to the parents as possible.

Caregivers can change over time. Maybe in the beginning, getting parents organized and documented is a good fit for one sibling, but when the health issues blossom, maybe someone else is just better at dealing with it. Life may take one caregiver out of the equation for whatever reason. Major caregiver is a tough role. It isn't a job to take on lightly, nor should it become the object of criticism for those who are not the major caregiver. It may take working together as siblings more than ever and squashing those sibling rivalries at this time.

Remember: if you have thirteen years of caregiving ahead of you, there is time to gather and understand the information regarding your parents' lives. There is time to accept the situation. The daily living scenario will take the most time, and it will change over the course of caregiving. If you've already had your first crisis, then concentrate on what was missing for that crisis—for example, financial info or health info. Do that first. Then just continue to fill in the blanks. The various chapters in this book cover the information you need to have in all of those areas.

Every time you are with your parents, try to find out something else. Have them tell you stories of their lives or their parents' lives. Ask them about their pensions or work or social life or what they did as a kid. How did their parents fare as they aged?

Hint: Do *not* treat them as children. They are not children. They are fully functioning adults who are losing capabilities. They have had a full life. This isn't a judgment about that life. It is about their decisions and where they find themselves now. Respect them.

Write everything down. There are some online sites that you can use to document your information. Be cautious. Find out how secure a site is. You don't want all your parents' information potentially hacked.

Carry a briefcase with the information that you require. During part of our caregiving activities, we carried a briefcase with the legal papers (powers of attorney, parents' driver licenses, phone numbers, and insurance papers) because it seemed that everywhere we turned, someone was asking for something. We carried a folder of phone numbers needed (doctor, lawyer, bank, neighbors). The phone numbers of neighbors became very important on a few occasions. If your parents are in a facility, some of those numbers may be helpful as well. The facility will have your and all the rest of the siblings' contact information. I was third in line for my folks, and I still got calls. I got calls when neither of my two siblings was available at the time. It happens. Make sure all pertinent people have all of your phone numbers.

This caregiving journey becomes a full-time job. Your regular full-time job becomes your respite from the caregiving job. Be watchful. As your caregiving activities increase and intensify, the first thoughts of the day and the last thoughts will be about your parents, what they are doing and how they are that day. It becomes all encompassing. Being far away from your parents does add stress.

The preparation outlined in these chapters will save you so much time, (I hope) prevent unnecessary crises, and relieve some stress. Why have an unnecessary crisis when there will be plenty of opportunities to have crises that you cannot prevent? Preparation and knowledge are what you need. Some of these preparations will even save you money.

Earlier, I mentioned that your relationship with your parents is somewhat immaterial as you handle the caregiving activities. If you doubt that statement, I have an example of a very brave caregiver that I know. If your relationship with your parents isn't so good, maybe this example will help you decide that the caregiving needed doesn't depend upon total respect or total love for your parents.

My husband and I noticed that an elderly gentleman wasn't doing so well, and we were concerned. Since we knew his family, we called one day to offer any help. *Besides, we thought, what's the worst that could happen?* They could tell us that it wasn't any of our business. We could help in a very real way if they did need it. I met with his family, and they were very grateful for our assistance. We outlined the critical things to get done immediately (health care power of attorney, HIPAA and financial power of attorney). These had to be redone. Those items were over thirty years old, and much had changed. The named executor had died, and the other children were over three thousand miles away and didn't communicate consistently. So changes were necessary.

The family had a poor relationship with this particular parent. However, they had been close to the deceased parent, and in honor of that parent, they kept track of the other parent. They would check in occasionally. By the time we started to help, the person was in terrible shape in every way, physically and financially. One of them said to me one day, "No one deserves to die this way."

We worked together and helped find resources that did help the parent and the family. This member of the family became the major caregiver for someone that he had little respect or regard for. But the parent was still worthy of help. This individual gave of himself out of respect for the individual. And the help was necessary.

Be mindful of the definitions of key terms used in this chapter:

Caregiving—Any help, assistance, direction, action, or facilitating that you do in support of your elderly parents.

Major caregiver--The spokesperson for the elderly parents and the first in line to be called when the various crises hit.

Afford—Amount of money, time, and involvement you can spend.

To Do:

1. Review the checklist in the introduction, and write down what you know and what you need to find out
2. Have a sibling meeting. Use the following agenda (it's the same as the agenda presented earlier in the chapter).
3. Commit to the caregiving.

Sibling Meeting Agenda

1. Objectives of Meeting
   a. Understand what each of you knows about your parents.
   b. Identify what each of you is able to do.
   c. Identify what you don't know about your parents.
   d. Identify what you cannot do, won't do, or don't want to do.
2. Guiding Principles of the Meeting
   a. *No judgements!*
   b. Keep your ego out of this meeting.
      Note: if you don't, the subsequent caregiving *will* remove all ego from your personality.
   c. All information is good.
   d. This isn't about power, control, or ego.
   e. Be honest with yourself and your siblings. As an example, if you really don't want your parents to move in with you, say so. It's not wrong.
3. List of Items that You Know About
   a. Use the checklist to begin.
   b. Assign unknown checklist items to individuals
   c. Decide how to document and communicate new information and who is responsible for doing so.
4. Priority Setting
   a. What's a critical item?
   b. If there are no critical items, start making the list from top to bottom.

      i.   Note: health care power of attorney and HIPAA forms, if not done, are the most critical.

     ii.   The general financial situation needs to be defined.

5. Communications setup

    a. How will you communicate?

    b. When? How much? Revise over time.

6. Assign the major caregiver role.

In preparation for this huge chapter and since I used to be a teacher, I am giving you a pop quiz. You have ten minutes. Put "Don't know" as an answer when appropriate.

Pop Quiz

1. What's the name of your parents' doctor(s)?

2. What type of doctors are they?

3. Do your parents have supplementary health insurance? What does it cost per month? Or do they have a Medicare Advantage Plan?

4. What do they pay monthly for drugs? (Include Part D and copays).

5. What drugs are they on? And why are they on them?

6. Which hospital do they go to?

7. Do they have a health care power of attorney?
   a. If "Yes" then, where is it kept? Have you read it? Who is the health care agent?
   b. If "No" then, when will you get it created?

3. Have you met your parents' doctors? What are their addresses? How long does it take to get to the office?

4. Do you have the HIPAA form signed?

CHAPTER 2
Health

So how did you do on the quiz? Don't worry; I won't collect it. This quiz starts you knowing about your parents' health care situation. It may be a painful reminder of how little you know, but it's a beginning. You need to know the answers to those questions. You do not have to get all the answers at the same time.

I once gave this quiz in a class I taught on caregiving. I was amazed by how little these very caring and thoughtful people knew about their parents. Then I thought of myself before caregiving started—I was the same. I didn't know a thing. I didn't know the names of my parents' doctors or what drugs they took. Initially, my parents did not have health care powers of attorney, but we fixed that.

There are many aspects of the health care surrounding your parents. You must understand the state of your parents' health. You must know what conditions, diseases, and drugs they have. How can you help support them without knowing that information? How can you help them, yourself, and your family make the best decisions you can unless you have the facts?

Advice: Attend meetings with doctors, nurses, therapists, and any other medical professional your folks go to. Take notes during the meetings. This is critical. Your attendance shows the medical support team that you are engaged. It helps them put a face to the support your parents need, and it gives you an opportunity to know the level of care that your parents are getting.

Knowledge of your parents' medical support team is critical as the needs increase and when there is a medical crisis. Take the day off of work sometime, and drive your folks to the appointments. Experience what they experience—the time it takes to get to the clinic, how they are treated, what the doctor or nurses look like, and how easy is it for your folks to get around. Take the same route they take. Find out which pharmacy they go to. Is it close?

The Basics

You don't have to be a medical professional to help your folks out medically. You do have to know their medical support team and what their situation is. Knowing your parents' situation means knowing what conditions/diseases they have, what drugs they take, what health needs they have (inhaler, cane, pacemaker, and so on), and what their medical schedule is. By medical schedule, I mean their appointment times, scheduled visits, medication requirements (time of day and quantity), in-home visits, and treatment times and durations.

Create a document with the names of the doctors and their phone numbers. Your parents may have more than one doctor—the regular physician and specialists, depending upon their medical situation. Next to the names of the doctors write down the names of the clinics and their addresses and phone numbers. As an example, my father-in-law had four doctors. We got to know those doctors well as we moved through my father-in-law's medical situation. Share this information with all concerned, and maybe post it on the refrigerator. Create a calendar with medical appointments and schedules.

What kind of doctor is their regular doctor? An internist, family doctor, or gerontologist? If at all possible, switch the main doctor to a gerontologist. They aren't available everywhere. If you can't find one labeled such, there may be a doctor who specializes in elder care in your area. A gerontologist only works with people who are seventy-five years or older. The needs are different at that age. The gerontologist and the staff know older people. Gerontologists specialize in the care of elderly patients, just like a pediatrician specializes in the care of children. Gerontologists understand old age. They know the research, they know how drugs affect older adults, and most important, they understand and know Medicare (medical insurance for people over sixty-five). They understand how to talk to the Medicare folks, and they know how to write prescriptions so that Medicare approves the payments. They know what they can and cannot do to maximize Medicare. Medicare has many rules. If you don't work in the field every day, you don't learn them all. Gerontologists and their staff work with Medicare every day. They know how to follow the rules established by Medicare.

They understand supplemental health care plans and Medicare Advantage Plans and know what the restrictions are. They get old age.

Definition

Medicare—Federal-government-subsidized medical insurance for United States citizens sixty-five and older. Medicare is funded by contributions from workers and through monthly premiums from the over-sixty-five crowd. Medicare is health insurance. It is not dental insurance, vision insurance, or long-term care insurance. It doesn't cover everything, just like most health insurance plans. It does *not* pay for nursing home costs. Medicare has deductibles and copays and, depending on the service, may only pay a portion of the bill. Medicare can be supplemented by either Medicare supplemental plans (provided by private insurance companies) or a Medicare Advantage Plan (pools of Medicare premiums reorganized to provide different benefits to subscribers). And there is a prescription drug piece to Medicare, called Medicare Part D. Depending on the drug plan your parents choose, the costs can be significantly different.

Medicaid is *not* Medicare. They are two different things. Medicaid will be covered in chapters 4 and 5 about financial and legal issues.

Find out whether your folks have a Medicare Advantage Plan or Medicare supplemental plan and which Part D (prescription drug) plan they have. What do they pay for those? If they don't have one and can afford it, they should enroll in a supplemental plan. It will help cover the costs of what Medicare doesn't cover. The government's website, www.medicare.gov, has all the information about Medicare, including what Medicare covers and what it does not cover.

Make a list of their drugs. Look them up and find out what they do and the side effects. Talk to their doctors, nurses, and pharmacist regarding the medications. Make sure your folks are taking the drugs recommended and taking them appropriately (with or without food, at the right time of day, and so on). Count the pills when you visit, or talk to the pharmacy for packaging options to make it easier for your parents to keep track of their medications. Keep the list of drugs with you at all times. This document becomes critical when an emergency happens. They may be taken to a hospital or an emergency center where their normal medical team is not handling their care. The doctors and nurses need to know what medications they are taking.

Also note which vitamins, supplements, and herbal remedies they take. These have the potential to interact with regular drugs so you will want to know and their doctor wants to know.

One item that became very useful for us was an emergency information document that we posted on my in-laws' refrigerator. When the nine-one-one calls happened, the responders could take that document and know immediately what the situation was. The document should have the name of their main doctor, the hospital they go to, the drugs they take, and the main contact in your family for emergencies. Post this on the refrigerator or some other place within easy view of emergency staff. Most likely, at some time, either you, your parents' neighbors, or your parents will call nine-one-one. Encase the paper within a plastic bag to protect it, and update it as the situation changes.

Here is an example:

Emergency Information
John Parent, born 1928

Physician: Dr. David Jones, Health Care Clinic, 352-1111
Hospital: St. Ignatius, 352-1112
General Health: uses walker (hip replacement), Hodgkin's lymphoma
Medications: prednisone, colchicine
Supplements: General vitamin, calcium supplement
Allergies: penicillin, wheat
Insurance: Medicare and supplemental health insurance
Wears glasses
DPOA, HCPOA, Main contact: Lisa, daughter, Middletown, IA—607-888-1111

This piece of paper cuts through to essential information for emergency workers. They will appreciate it, and so will you. It will help prevent mistakes because during a crisis, incorrect and mostly incomplete information is usually given by the parent or the spouse.

Do your parents go to a dentist? Who is it, and where is it? Do they go regularly? Dental health sometimes gets lost in the shuffle with other major health issues. It was a dentist who recognized the seriousness of my father-in-law's situation.

Another item to know is your parents' past history: operations, conditions, issues, accidents, and so on. My mother had had tuberculosis as a child. It was mild but nonetheless an important fact to know and give to the nursing home that she went to. All nursing homes test for TB upon entry. Well, my mother always tested positive for TB. It was a good thing to know so no one would get too excited.

Summary of the Basics

1. Gather the information about the doctors: name, address, phone, and specialty.
2. Find out if your parents have a supplemental (or advantage) plan and what they pay for it.
3. Document the drugs that they are on.
4. Create an emergency document for posting in the house.

Next, we cover essential, critical documents that all adults should have and the reasons these are so important.

Documents

HIPAA

While at the doctors, if not before, get the HIPAA form signed. This allows you to ask questions of the doctors and call for information. This is not about making decisions; this is about getting the information that you need to help your parents in the best way possible.

HIPAA is a privacy authorization form. HIPAA is the abbreviation for Health Insurance Portability and Accountability Act. This act was passed in 1996. Embedded within the legislation was medical information privacy. Your parents signing this form allows you to call their medical support team to get information about them. How else can you expect to understand what is going on medically? Can you rely on your parents to tell you the facts? Do they remember the facts? Do they understand what the doctors are telling them?

Every doctor's office and hospital have their version of a HIPAA form. Most physicians and hospitals now, as a matter of course, have the HIPAA signed right away, the first time you come in. If your parents have been going to the same doctor or clinic for a while, it may have slipped through the cracks. So check on it. Call the doctor's office and see if you are authorized to ask questions regarding your parents.

Your parents do need to agree to have your name (and you must sign it) on this form. In one family, the father refused to have his son on the form. However, that son, being diplomatic, took his father to the doctor one day and in front of the doctor asked about HIPAA. The father couldn't lose face in front of the doctor, so he agreed to let his son be authorized for HIPAA. That's one way to get the HIPAA form signed. The HIPAA form allows you to gather information. You will need it on an ongoing basis. If you are a long-distance caregiver, it becomes even more critical. You can call and get the information you need. Some parents don't share information well, and sometimes they just don't hear or understand what they are being told. They could also be overwhelmed. Having your name on the HIPAA form also shows the medical support team that the family members are concerned and involved. They get to know you and know what you need to understand.

Another reason for going to the doctor with your folks is that they may not hear everything the doctor says. They may also forget—either really or expeditiously—everything the doctor says. If you want to support your folks, then you need to understand what the doctors are telling them, why they are saying it, and what follow-up needs to be done. The medical staff needs your support in the follow-throughs when your parents go back home. Parents do often need help in understanding the medical advice and following it. And some parents do not like you knowing. Frankly, I didn't want to know everything that was wrong. But I had to. And so do you. If your parents are miffed at this, then so be it. They will continue to be angry, surly, or crabby with you. You just have to accept it and take it. Always keep in mind the goal is making decisions that are in the best interests of your parents and supporting them the best way you can. To do that, you need to get information and data. If they get angry at you, then they just get angry. This isn't about you.

Notice the interactions that your parents have with the doctor. How does the doctor deal with them? If you become uncomfortable with the doctor, change doctors. I helped someone change doctors because she attended a meeting with her parent and was appalled by the doctor's discussion and behavior. Ask yourself, "What is the best care that can be given to my parent? Is the current doctor the best one for my parent at this time?"

Keeping track of your folks' medications can help prevent serious issues down the road. A consulting pharmacist who works with the elderly has stated in studies that he has done, that if older folks are on at least eight medications, there is a 100 percent chance that they will have a fall. The falls are created in part because of the interactions of all the medications that they are taking. Falls are critical events in elders' lives. They are a reason they go into hospitals and subsequently into rehab centers. It's a very difficult time in their lives. So why not prevent as many falls as possible? Understand the drugs and their effects, and help monitor their usage. Maybe it's time for them to get off some of the drugs. You cannot make that decision though. You need to employ a consulting pharmacist and obviously your parents' medical team to help you with this. A consulting pharmacist's objective view of the medications can help you understand both your parents' situation and how to monitor the drugs and their effects. Make this an annual evaluation. It also helps doctors, who have so many patients they can't keep track of everything. They appreciate the involvement.

When you are at your parents' home, check their medications. Are they taking them? Are they taking them at the right time of day and the right dosage? Call their pharmacy to see if there is some packaging that makes this easier for them. My mother, who had dementia, had always given my dad his medications. Well, in her dementia, she would change Dad's meds at her will. So we had the pharmacist repackage the meds in plastic containers with days and a.m. or p.m. marked. It, for whatever reason, prevented my mother from giving my dad his medications in the wrong way. We found out she had been changing his medications because my sister counted the pills. At times, a significant number of pills were missing, and at others, too many pills remained. This situation showed us that the normal living habits of your folks may sometimes interfere with their health. It seems normal to them, and they don't question it. Sometimes it gets dangerous. So every time any of us went to see the folks, we counted pills. Just another caregiving activity to keep you busy!

Health Care Power of Attorney (HCPOA)

Get one!

This is critical. Unlike a HIPAA form, this is a decision-making document. However, older people sometimes refuse to get one created because they think or are afraid that someone is going to throw them into a nursing home or pull the plug before they are ready. If this were a reasonable fear, the named health care agent should never have been appointed in the first place. The parent names the agent and entrusts the agent to execute whatever his or her wishes are. This can get very emotional.

Most states have a generic HCPOA on the health and human services (or whatever they are called locally) website. If you go to that website, you can print off the document and fill in the blanks. Follow the directions that the website provides. The HCPOA does have to be witnessed for it to be legal. If the generic HCPOA from the state's health and human services website does not satisfy you, see an attorney specializing in elder law. He or she will provide you with a customized, detailed HCPOA. HCPOAs do not cost a lot of money, and some lawyers charge a flat rate for them (e.g., $100). It's worth the money and the time. Please do this. Keep in mind that a HCPOA is *not* a financial power of attorney. You cannot make any financial decisions through a HCPOA.

First of all, if you approach HCPOA properly, it's the person creating the HCPOA who is truly making the decisions. He or she is retaining control of how he or she wants things to proceed and making the decisions, not a health care agent, not the hospital staff, and not the Supreme Court. The individual is making his or her own decisions. The agent carries out the decisions. No HCPOA can account for every conceivable occurrence. So the agent may have to choose options, depending on how generic the HCPOA is.

The HCPOA saves time, money, and stress. Issues occur, and incapacitation happens. If an issue occurs and the elderly person is unable to communicate what he or she wants (for example, in the case of stroke, heart attack, or dementia), then the doctors declare that person unable to make his or her own decisions. The health care agent is then the one doing the communicating, not making the decisions.

The HCPOA can be changed as often as the individual wants to. It just needs to have witnesses sign it to make it legitimate, or it may require a notary. Your state will have its particular rules. You need to understand what those rules are. Health care professionals want to and need to know what type of process they may need to embark upon. They can take very extraordinary measures to keep someone alive. If the individual wants this, then he or she should put it in the HCPOA. Maybe the individual wants less extraordinary measures; then he or she should put that in the HCPOA so everyone understands.

The HCPOA can and should change over time. You may want something completely different at forty than you want at ninety. Review it, and modify it whenever the situation warrants or every ten years.

Also, be sure to *read* it. Know who the health care agent is. Did that person move? Is that person still appropriate? If not, get it changed. People move, and they don't stay in touch. The health care agent is not necessarily the executor of a will. Those can be two different people. Declaring an executor is *not* declaring a health care agent or vice versa. If you are the health care agent, you should have a copy of the HCPOA. If not, get one. You also need to understand what your job is.

One of my clients asked me a question about six months after our work was completed. She asked, "Where is the HCPOA kept?"

I responded, "Don't you have a copy? You're the health care agent!"

She said she didn't have a copy. I told her to get one and who probably had a copy.

You should also know what the health care power of attorney states the process for declaring a person incapable of making his or her own health care decisions. Typically, it's two doctors who examine the person and sign an affidavit. In one case, the individuals had waived the two physician requirement. In their HCPOA (and this is true), they had statements that they would declare each other incompetent. Yes, one of the pair had dementia and was surely going to declare the other incompetent. The other spouse was trying desperately to keep everything the same as it always had been and was never going to declare his wife incompetent. This was wrong, horribly wrong and dangerous.

Ego check: Don't wish to be a health care agent; it isn't fun. You are the one who will be getting the calls.

You can get a HCPOA set up where more than one person has equal say. We ended up with that with the in-laws, so my husband and his brother could each make decisions when necessary. We were both long-distance from the in-laws, so it made sense. But make sure that each of you understands what is in the HCPOA and what measures will or will not be taken. Your understanding has to be the same. This doesn't mean that you shouldn't consult other family members. If there is time, always let others know what is about to take place. During an emergency, obviously since time is of the essence, the decisions have to be made right away. Communicate those decisions as soon as you can.

A question people forget to ask is, "What if I don't have a health care power of attorney? What happens?" It'll cost you money when the incapacitation occurs.

True story: A friend of mine had financial power of attorney. She stated that her mother had created the health care power of attorney and she was the agent. She didn't have a copy of the HCPOA but was sure there was one. Her mother voluntarily moved into assisted living. While there, about three weeks later, her mother had a major issue. The assisted-living facility transported her mother to the hospital.

Note: assisted-living facilities do not have skilled nursing care on duty at all times.

The family couldn't find the health care power of attorney. The doctor declared that her mother could not make her own decisions. A second doctor reviewed her mother's situation and declared her incompetent as well. As a result, the assisted living facility would not take her back. The mother had to go to a nursing home.

What was the option? In order for the mother to go to the nursing home, a guardian had to make that decision. The daughter had to hire an attorney (and a second attorney was appointed for her mother). Since the mother was declared incompetent and there was no HCPOA, the *only* recourse available to this caring, involved, doing-more-than-her-share caregiver was to go to court and become her guardian—yes, a court appearance, two lawyers, a second medical opinion, and about three thousand dollars out of her pocket. Why spend thousands of dollars if you can do a HCPOA for free? People! It is your responsibility, and it's *your* money. Just so you know, if you do become a guardian of person, every year after your parent is placed in a nursing home, the state reviews the situation. So into court, every year afterward, the two lawyers, a representative from the state, possibly you, and possibly your parent go, and guess who gets to pay for it all? *You*, the guardian. Such a waste of time and money! Three thousand versus nothing. You choose.

The HCPOA can have a stipulation that states that the health care agent can decide to put you into a care facility. *Care facilities* include a wider range of facilities than just nursing homes, including assisted living facilities and memory care facilities. Medicare does not pay for these services. If the parent is indigent, he or she can get on Medicaid (called different things in different states), and Medicaid will pay for either in-home nursing care or nursing home care. Medicaid will not pay for assisted living.

Let's recap.

Develop these three documents:

1. Emergency information document to be posted in the house, containing the basic information of the parents.
2. HIPAA form—get the form signed and established at all clinics and hospitals so that you can gather information about the health environment of your parents.
3. Health care power of attorney—establish one. Don't wait. It's too critical and costly if you do not establish one.

Another issue that you have to face is understanding the medical terminology. You need to understand what the doctor is saying. So ask questions, look it up, or adopt a nurse into your family. Usually we hear what is being said and think that we understand, but later, when reviewing, we discover we've missed important implications. We may not understand the gravity of what was said or the appropriate actions to take based on what was said. We may not understand the situation well enough to communicate with other family members. You need to ask and make sure that you are clear.

The following example demonstrates the importance of understanding terminology. During one incident we faced, we were in a serious medical conversation, and neither of us understood a particular comment that the doctor made. We were committed to helping our parents, and we had been through a lot already, so we knew a lot. But …

My father-in-law had been diagnosed with stage-four cancer. Serious stuff. We attended the meeting with the doctor to review the test results and to understand what the prognosis and treatment plan would be. I went along to be a witness, write notes, and watch out for my mother-in-law, who was in mid-stage Alzheimer's. My mother-in-law fell asleep. My husband was conversing with the doctor, asking questions, and listening intently. My father-in-law wasn't getting the majority of what was being said. I was taking notes. The next day, I asked my husband, "What's palliative care?" and he said he didn't know.

I said, "But it's in my notes and I remember her [the doctor] saying it—I thought you understood."

He asked, "What else is in the notes?"

Within those twenty-four hours since the meeting, my husband could not remember 40 percent of what I had written down. We didn't understand the phrase *palliative care*. We are both intelligent, involved, committed people, and the presiding doctor was clear and precise and took time with us. So why didn't we understand?

The first time you hear something, you may not understand the implications of what is being said. Because you have the HIPAA form signed, you can call the doctor and ask for clarification. You need to do that to be the best support for your parents and to be able to clearly communicate the situation to your siblings or other family members.

Pay attention, take notes (or have someone take notes), and ask questions so that you fully understand and can support your parents effectively. Be prepared not to remember everything. If you can't remember, how is your parent supposed to remember? In that same meeting, my father-in-law didn't remember (or chose not to) several operations he had had, didn't know how much he weighed (even though his weight was taken five minutes earlier), and took out his ever-present list of questions to ask the doctor. That list followed him to every doctor he was seeing. The questions never changed. It is hard to comprehend everything. It is hard to take in information in a technical language that you are not well-versed in. Don't beat yourself up; just follow up with the doctor for your questions or concerns.

Document calls, conversations, and discussions, and communicate the information to your siblings. Don't exclude them. It's up to you to keep them informed regardless of their reaction to it. If you are the major caregiver for your parents, it is your responsibility to communicate through e-mails, phone conversations, or even in online medical tracking sites that help keep all informed.

Many times, it's what isn't said that masks an issue or masks the seriousness of an issue. Stating that a particular disease is 90 percent curable is a fact for some cases and is true of some cancers. It's a wonderful piece of information. Except, you have to ask what isn't stated. What's the treatment? Can the individual withstand the treatment? If not, then the individual is in the 10 percent that won't be cured. Too many times, we simply accept the statements and do not question them. We're not trying to challenge; we're trying to understand. Get used to discerning the information that is given and some that is not given. Look at yourself and see what assumptions you are making. This is where the HIPAA signatures come into play. You can call the doctors, nurses, and pharmacist and get the information that you need. Typically, it's the implications that are obscure. Your understanding of the implications will determine how you care for your parents and how you support them. It leads to what will be needed or what needs to be planned for.

So what is palliative care? The older we get, the less able we are to withstand certain treatments. Many times, the medical profession will do *palliative* care and rightly so. That's managing symptoms, pain, and discomfort but not curing an issue. You need to understand that to accept the prognosis as well as to help your parents (and the rest of the family) accept it as well. You need to understand what is going to happen and support those who need the support.

Following is a brief discussion of the different types of facilities. This is not an exhaustive list of the capabilities of each. Over time, these facilities do change. As you visit facilities, ask questions about their capabilities, what they provide, and also what they do not provide.

Facilities

I've been mentioning certain types of facilities without definition. In general, the arrangements are as follows. Your area may not have all of these.

- elder housing
- assisted living
- group homes
- memory care
- nursing homes
- rehab centers

The current older population doesn't always understand the wide variety of housing arrangements that are available. Between assisted living places, group homes, memory care facilities, and yes, nursing homes, there is a scalable way to get additional help. Just go see a few places. You would be surprised how wonderful many facilities are. I've listed some prices, but do not assume those prices are set. Many geographic locations have a wider range of prices. The prices given are there to set an expectation for you. The actual prices can be higher or lower, depending on the location, services, and quality of the facility.

Advice: Go to some facilities with your parents. Get them introduced to what's available. They may be pleasantly surprised, and they may even know someone there.

Notice how the staff interacts with the residents. I believe that the facility offers a new home for the individual. The staff should be treating the residents as if they are in their home. The staff works in that facility, but the individual lives there.

I've had people tell me that they will never place their parent in a nursing home. Don't make promises that you can't keep. If there is dementia, at some point, the person may have to go into a facility. And it might be after you, the caregiver collapse and become so ill yourself (or die) that the only recourse is to put the individual in a facility. If you don't do it, the state *may* come in for safety reasons—safety of the individual or the neighborhood—and may take control and place your parent in a facility. If the parent has dementia and tries to burn down the house, that's a safety issue. States have different laws regarding the placement of a person into a facility. You need to know what your state can or will do. You need to be prepared for that.

Definitions

Elder housing typically means condos or apartments that have a lower age limit attached to them (over fifty-fifty, as an example). They do not provide any nursing but do provide a community for the above middle-aged. Sometimes this housing is connected with a facility that provides the full range of help that might be needed as time goes on. Those types of arrangements are convenient because the move to an assisted living facility or nursing home isn't as abrupt and disruptive and the surroundings are familiar to the individual. Rent and purchase prices vary greatly. These facilities often offer social events and a variety of interactions to keep the elder crowd busy and engaged.

Assisted living, approximately $3,500 per month, provides both a safety net and independence for a wide swath of the elderly population. It is a step up from an independent facility. Assisted living places offer security, some personal attention and help, meals, and activities, like in elder housing. They also provide a community within which the parent lives for company. The apartments are furnished with the person's own stuff, and the person can lock his or her doors. Employees have passkeys for emergencies. They have limited nursing care but may provide transportation to and from doctors' offices. Some assisted living facilities have a flat rate with a scalable rate for more help needed, or they may be a la carte. You decide if you want one, two, or three meals and a half hour of help getting up in the morning or one hour of help. Make an appointment to visit a few facilities in your parents' area. If dementia is involved, find out if the facility does any work with dementia. Otherwise, your parent may not be able to go there.

Group homes are similar in nature to assisted living facilities. Each individual has his or her own room, not an apartment. Some are established in a large home. With group homes, all residents congregate for meals and socializing. The individuals help with meal preparation, cleaning, and activities. There are group homes that cater to a specific group of people, e.g., Korean War veterans. The level of nursing help is limited. The cost is similar to assisted living facilities and in some cases may be slightly less.

Memory care facilities focus on dementia patients. Typically, but not always, they do not have nursing home (skilled nursing care) capability. They work with individuals with activities and brain exercises and provide a safe, comfortable environment for the individuals. When someone with dementia enters any facility, there will be a transition phase and that will most likely take at least three months. In that time, the person with dementia may be uncooperative, surly, or belligerent. They feel insecure in the unfamiliar surroundings. Once that transition takes place, the individual will settle into the routine. Dementia patients like routine and sameness. They do not and cannot cope with change. Memory care facilities range from $5,500 to $7,000 per month. Memory care facilities may be a part of a larger complex that includes a nursing home.

Nursing homes provide skilled nursing care for those elderly (or younger) who cannot in any way take care of themselves or have a need for significant care. Nursing homes cost on average $6,800 per month and higher. They are staffed with registered nurses and provide some activities but are concentrated on caring for the severely incapacitated folks.

Rehab Centers
Not always, but sometimes rehab centers are embedded within a nursing home. These centers provide a wide range of help (occupational, physical, and speech therapies) to rehabilitate someone after an accident or surgery. Rehab centers are not

concerned with just the elderly. These centers are trying to get the person back to his or her general condition before he or she entered a hospital (e.g., for a double-knee replacement). These are typically shorter-term stays. Medicare pays for rehab centers up to a point. It does not pay for any of the other types of facilities. There is a limit on the number of days (one hundred). If you are staying at a rehab center for more than a hundred days, you are living there. That's not a short-term stay. The rules change for Medicare payments. You need to check with the doctors or their staff and the facility to understand what Medicare will pay for.

If you have multiple rehab centers in your area, visit them. In one case, we visited four rehab centers for my folks. Three of them were awful. If you wouldn't want to go there, why would you place your parent there? Parents may believe that rehab centers are nursing homes. The fact that rehab centers are usually placed within a nursing home is hard to dispute. However, rehab centers aren't for long-term stays. Picking out a rehab center may seem to be not very high on your list, but if there are choices in your area, pick one out. In the section on hospitals, we talk about how knowing which rehab center your parent will go to becomes critical. Know ahead of time where you will be placing your parent. It will save you an incredible amount of stress if you choose a facility ahead of time. All facilities will set up appointments on weekends. They know that you work and can't get there during the week. They are very accommodating.

An organization I worked with very successfully and used personally was "A Place for Mom." This 800 phone service will find options for you based on your conditions (e.g., memory care). They will set up appointments for you, follow up with you, and give you some general useful information. A Place for Mom is a nationwide organization.

Note: A Place for Mom gets paid by the facility. You do not pay, but you should know that this is the arrangement. I found them wonderful to work with and very knowledgeable about not only facilities but also other elder issues.

Your responsibilities do not end with the parent entering a facility. Some of your concerns will be alleviated (medical management, safety, nutrition, and cleanliness). However, you still have the obligation to see that your parents are well taken care of: understand the scope of the help, meet the staff, and monitor your parents' health and wellness. Drop in unannounced and watch how things operate. Find out what food they are given, what activities are done, and what programs are planned. Participate in family programs whenever possible and meet other caregivers. Always participate in and be available for the care consultations. These meetings between the facility administrator, support team in the facility, and the family should happen on a regular basis. Initially, it may happen monthly for three to six months and afterward possibly quarterly. If you're long-distance, they happen over the phone.

Hospice Care

Hospice is a Medicare-funded service that provides care to the person who is dying. Hospice care can occur in a special hospice-care facility or be done in-home (or in-facility). They provide an incredible array of helpful, caring, respectful palliative options. When it becomes too much for you to care for your parent in-home or he or she requires more attention than a nursing home can give, call in hospice. There are conditions under which hospice will come in so you need to be aware of what those parameters are. Typically, but not always, death must be a possibility within six months. Hospice is available for advanced dementia patients and can provide significant support for the loved one. There are for-profit and not-for-profit hospice organizations. The preference should be for how comfortable you feel with the organization, not whether their organization is a for-profit entity or not.

Here's some of what Medicare pays. Please note that the rules change frequently. This is what is current at the time of publication. It may be different by the time you read this! All of these numbers were taken from www.medicare.gov.

- Hospital stays—The amount covered depends on how long you're in the hospital. In 2013, for the first sixty days, you pay a maximum of $1,184 and Medicare pays the rest. After that, the longer you stay, the more you pay. You pay $296 per day for days 61 through 90. After that, you pay $592 per day until the sixty days of "lifetime benefits" run out. Then you pay all the costs.

- Skilled nursing facility care (rehab)—This is to allow you to recover after a stay in the hospital. Medicare does not pay for long stays in a nursing facility. It pays for the first twenty days. From the twenty-first to one-hundredth day, you pay a copay of $148 per day. After that, you pay all the costs of your stay in a skilled nursing facility.

- Home health care—If you are recovering from an illness or injury and your doctor says you need short-term skilled care, Medicare Part A pays for nurses and some therapists to provide services in your home. As long as the treatment is Medicare-approved and the provider is certified by Medicare, you pay nothing, except for 20 percent of the Medicare-approved amount for some medical equipment, such as wheelchairs and walkers. At times, Medicare *may* pay for the rental of a wheelchair. However, if the physical therapist puts down a goal of walking three hundred steps a day, then Medicare will refuse to pay the rental and you will have to either rent or purchase the wheelchair.

- Hospice care—This covers some care for people who are terminally ill. Medicare Part A covers most drug costs, as well as medical and support services. Hospice care is usually given at home or in the facility where you live. But Medicare also covers most of the charges for short stretches in a hospice facility to manage pain and other symptoms and to give the regular caregiver a break. There may be a five-dollar maximum copay per prescription for outpatient drugs for pain and symptom management, and you pay 5 percent of the approved Medicare amount for inpatient respite care services.

- Blood transfusions—After you pay for the first three pints, Medicare Part A pays 80 percent of any additional blood you need in the hospital. In most cases, the hospital gets blood from a blood bank at no charge, and you won't have to pay for it or replace it. If the hospital has to buy blood for you, you must either pay the hospital's costs for the first three units of blood you get in a calendar year or have the blood donated.

Facilities cost lots of money, but sometimes they are the only option for the family. Nursing an elderly, failing individual is a full-time job. And it frequently comes with medical interaction (emptying the colostomy bag). It's not for everyone. There is a lot of in-home help you can engage from companionship all to way to nursing help. There are also many modifications you can do to the home to assist in handling the physical needs of the patient. Visiting medical supply companies or home modification businesses can help you understand the incredible array of physical help that is out there. From step-in showers (versus a step-over-the-tub shower) to installation of a fully automated harness system, the options may be cheaper and helpful for a while. The installation of an automated chair that goes up the stairs costs about twelve thousand dollars. But if your parents' house has two stories and the parent has difficulty negotiating the stairs, a one-time installation that costs $12,000 is cheaper than three months of staying at an assisted living facility. It may be worth the investment. It gives the individual a sense of independence.

There are a plethora of in-home help businesses catering to the elderly. In-home help is usually of two types: non-medical help and medical help. We hired both types for my parents and in-laws. Some can do light housekeeping, prepare a meal or two, or administer medical shots and do procedures in the home. Prices range from twenty-five to forty dollars per hour, depending on the level of medical help required. A lot of them require a minimum of three hours of help. In one situation with my father-in-law, who needed daily radiation treatments for six weeks, we hired a wonderful organization and the woman came four days a week, got my father-in-law and mother-in-law to the hospital for the radiation treatment, got them home, and prepared a simple meal for them. We went on the fifth day because the doctor met with us at that time. As I stated earlier, we were long-distance and couldn't make the trip five days a week without quitting our jobs. In the next chapter, which is about daily living activities, I expand a bit more on in-home helpers. They are a way to keep the folks in their home for a longer period.

We fought both my parents and my in-laws every step of the way. They didn't want help, didn't want a stranger coming into the house, or felt that they were losing all of their independence and just couldn't face it. Help can give them more independence than they initially realize. Having someone (well-vetted) coming in can relieve some stress for your parents. Prior to this, your parents had kept their house or apartment, had done all the shopping, and had done all the upkeep. But now, they aren't capable anymore. Help can free them. Help can let them continue their independence. Everyone needs help along the way. It doesn't mean he or she is giving up necessarily. It is hard to admit that your parents are old, and they aren't admitting it to themselves. Part of that is okay. But when it gets to losing nine pounds in one month for one of the parents and then establishing Meals on Wheels over parental objections, it relieves both the caregivers and the parents tremendously. They got a full meal that was well-balanced and nutritious (although my father said to get the salt shaker out). It relieved some stress for the family because someone was walking into the house every day. It relieved stress because we knew that our parents were getting a hot, nutritious meal every day.

Do your parents have long-term-care insurance? You need to find out. Long-term care insurance can help pay for both in-home medical help and facility costs, depending on the policy and the cost. It's cheaper the younger you are when you purchase it. Long-term care insurance can help relieve some of the costs. It won't cover everything, but it does get you partway there. It is a monthly expense, so that needs to be weighed with potential benefits down the road.

Is one of your parents a veteran? Then you need to check out Aid and Attendance. This is a military benefit targeted at helping veterans with medical expenses as they age. It can help cover the in-home help or facility cost help. There are income restrictions and estate value restrictions. But it is there. I recommend going to a financial adviser who specializes in the elderly; they can help you with the application. It's worth doing, and the financial adviser cannot charge you anything for this application. In some areas, the county's veterans' department can help too. This benefit for a long time was not well-advertised. But different organizations that work with the elderly are educating people on this benefit. We didn't know about it for either set of parents. My father for sure would have qualified. Again, it's called Aid and Attendance. You can go to the Veterans Administration website to find out more about it.

Hospitals

There are several types of hospitals now. The ones most of us relate to are the acute care hospitals. Depending on your area, that may be the only type of hospital. Larger metro areas may have chronic conditions or diseases hospitals. These are not nursing homes but hospitals that you are expected to leave. If your condition is chronic and needs constant monitoring or adjusting, these hospitals aren't as expensive as the acute care.

For the acute care hospitals, their mission is to alleviate or cure your condition or your disease. This is where the emergency rooms are. If your parent falls down and breaks a hip, he or she will go to an acute care hospital where they will analyze, diagnose, and treat the immediate issue. Then the parent has to leave. These hospitals are not long-term-stay places. The reimbursement that Medicare pays to hospitals is less than their cost of keeping you there. The supplemental or advantage plan may provide more dollars to the hospital. A few years ago, the average daily cost for a room at a hospital in the Midwest was about $1,600 a day.

When your parent enters the hospital, the medical team there will not be the regular team your parent is used to. They need to know immediately what the health situation is for your parent. You can help them out tremendously if you have the information. If you have copies of medical information for your parents or copies of medical reports and testing, include them in the briefcase full of other useful information.

Example

In one case, an elderly parent was admitted to the hospital for a very bad infection. The admitting doctor recognized some symptoms unrelated to the infection. The family had kept the documentation from a very recent diagnosis. This was a new hospital, a new team, and not the set of doctors that the family had been working with. The family was able to provide the most recent report and help the new set of doctors with their analysis.

It's important to keep the records. It can help.

Note: Medicare does not pay for subsequent nursing home placements from a hospital stay that is designated for "observation" or for "outpatient."

Back to what you need to be prepared for. Earlier in this chapter, I stated that you need to find a rehab center before your parent needs one. Here's why. Once in the hospital, you will be greeted by a social worker. That social worker's job is to keep you informed about the processes at the hospital, including the discharge. The social worker may state that your parent has a discharge team. If your parent cannot go home, he or she will have to go to a rehab center. If he or she breaks a hip or a leg, he or she could use some time and attention from the medical staff. That isn't coming from the hospital. They've taken care of the immediate issue.

Now it's time to discharge your parent. You will be told that there will be a care assessment meeting regarding your parent and decisions will be made in that meeting. (Are they ready to go home? What are the follow-up care and instructions?) All good stuff. Then the social worker's duty is to call you and tell you the decisions. True story again: they call you at work at 4:00 p.m. and state, "We are discharging your parent at 10:00 a.m. tomorrow morning. Where are they going?" This is stated definitively, assertively, and without question. You of course are pretty stressed; you have no idea where the parent is going. You probably will have to take another day off of work.

That's where the rehab center comes in to play. "Where are they going?" You are expected to have an answer because your parent is coming out of the hospital at 10:00 a.m. The second most asked question I ever got was, "Can they just discharge my parent?" And the answer is "No." Medicare law prohibits it. But the hospital has to discharge your parent. It's costing them money, and they don't do long-term non-acute care. The hospital will put pressure on you to answer the question. Since you've just gone through this crisis, you've taken time off of work, you are worried, and you haven't had time to look for a rehab. You barely know what it is. So find one ahead of time. You cannot change the rules or the hospitals. Save yourself a lot of grief and have *the name of a rehab ahead of time*. Even give it to the hospital staff so when they have their meeting, they have the name of the specific rehab center. The hospital can arrange transport to the rehab facility.

Some states may have a website service that lists all different types of facilities and what their services are to help you locate a rehab or other facility. It's a good place to start.

Medicaid

Medicaid in the United States is a social health care program for families and individuals with low income and resources. The web-site, Medicaid.gov, describes Medicaid as "Medicaid provides health coverage to millions of Americans, including eligible low-income adults, children, pregnant women, elderly adults and people with disabilities. Medicaid is administered by states, according to federal requirements. The program is funded jointly by states and the federal government."

Medicaid is the largest source of funding for medical and health-related services for people with low income in the United States. It is a means-tested program that is jointly funded by the state and federal governments and managed by the states, with each state currently having broad leeway to determine who is eligible for its implementation of the program. States are not required to participate in the program, although all currently do. Medicaid recipients must be US citizens or legal permanent residents and may include low-income adults, their children, and people with certain disabilities. Poverty alone does not necessarily qualify someone for Medicaid.

There are many rules associated with qualifying for Medicaid. It does pay for nursing home costs for those with no money. As I mentioned earlier, it is not Medicare. The social workers at facilities understand and typically are very helpful if you believe that your parent will eventually qualify for Medicaid.

Summary

- Go back to the pop quiz at the beginning of this chapter, and begin gathering and documenting all the answers to those questions.
- Get to know your parents' health situation.
- Create all documents (emergency, HCPOA, and HIPAA).
- Get to know your parents' health care team.
- Find a rehab center.
- Document all meetings with health care providers.
- If your parent is a veteran or veteran's spouse, check in to Aid and Attendance www.benefits.va.gov/PENSION/.

Home

During the last week of my mother's life, my two sisters, my husband, my brothers-in-law, and I sat in vigil with my mother. She had gone into a coma as a result of some physical incident. I don't know what the specifics were. She was ninety and had advanced dementia. She had been in a nursing home for three years. She was doing well there but had suffered a heart attack a year previous.

During my stage of the vigil, I got to know the nursing home so much better than on my other visits. Those visits were an hour or two or part of a facility celebration of some sort. My mother was a resident on the Alzheimer's ward, which housed ten residents. They each had their own room and their own bathroom. There was a general eating/activity area to the left of the locked door on this particular wing of the nursing home. They ate all their meals in the common room and had most of their activities there. The nursing home was much larger than just this wing.

The residents there were self-contained and didn't mix with the others in the nursing home except for programs or church services. This was a Catholic facility, and my mother was Lutheran. They did have Lutheran church services, and they would walk my mother down to the chapel to attend the Lutheran services.

Their world was small but safe and simple. The lives of the residents on this wing were based on simplicity, familiarity, and sameness. That's what dementia patients need.

So while I sat there for eight to nine hours on my vigil days, I got a deeper understanding of the routines. My mother was lying on her bed. The nursing staff would come in, move her around, wash her, and change her clothes. I would walk out of the room at that point. I heard the comings and goings of staff, shift changes, meal times, and activities.

Most of the time that I was in the room, I would have the door partially closed. One of the other residents, a fellow, would open the door wide. The first time he did that, it surprised me and I said something to him. But he wouldn't say anything or look at me; he would just open the door and then leave. It was obvious that my mother's door had to be wide open. He was one of the walkers. My mother was one of the walkers. They would walk up and down their hallway.

At other times, another resident—another walker—would come into the room. She spoke gibberish. You couldn't understand anything she said, but she still talked. I had no idea how to respond or say anything to her. She had been a resident there the whole time my mother was there. When I was shooed out of the room by the nurses, sometimes I'd see her walking and she would enter an empty room and look out a window. She would stand there for a while and just look at a world she could no longer comprehend. Then she would turn around and reenter the world she recognized. She visited my mother a lot.

One day, I was at my mother's bedside and I heard this shrieking laughter coming from the common room. I hadn't heard laughter on an Alzheimer's ward ever. Here the residents were all seated in a circle and tossing a huge, lightweight ball around. They were laughing. They were enjoying themselves. They were participating. My mother would have been there if she could have. She would have participated. That's when it hit me—this was my mother's home. She was cared for here. She had friends. She did stuff, and she had a good time. It wasn't just a nursing home. This had become my mother's home. What a gift we had been given.

CHAPTER 3
Daily Living

Activities of Daily Living (ADL)

Let's start with an example about what this means. Take yourself through *your* typical morning.

You wake up. It's about 6:30 a.m. You turn off the alarm, get up out of bed, go to the bathroom, brush your teeth, get the newspaper, open the newspaper, and read one thing. You get coffee ready, take a shower, get dressed, have breakfast, read more of the paper, and then fix lunch for yourself. You get in the car, drive to work, and think about what you have to do that day at work. It's now 8:00 a.m.

These are activities of daily living, just the normal, everyday stuff that you do. Now, let's translate these activities to someone who is in his or her eighties or nineties.

You wake up. You check to see if you are alive and then check to see if you can move. You need to get to the bathroom (or you use a urinal set next to your bed). You brush your teeth and maybe splash water on your face. You go to the kitchen, get your newspaper, read it, turn on the news, and have a piece of toast. Then you figure out what to do today, check your appointments, take your medications, and get dressed. Next, you lie down for a nap. It's now noon.

Everything takes longer. Everything is more of an effort. This is your parent. Your parent is slower. Your parent may also have some sort of disability or weakness. His or her day fills up with getting through the normal activities that we take for granted. He or she wonders why it feels like he or she hasn't done anything all day, and you wonder if he or she is going to make it through another day.

Observing an elder's daily life is so important to both understanding what he or she is feeling and what he or she is facing, each and every day. It's also important to understand what those challenges are and whether they can be mitigated somehow. It takes observation. Get all your siblings involved and compare notes. You may each notice something different. After I visited my folks, I would call my sister, who had the overall management of their care and tell her in detail what I observed, saw, and thought and what each parent did in the time that I was there. All those items I reported on were the daily doings of my parents.

Here's a list of some items to observe:

- When do they get up, nap, and go to bed?
- What do they eat and drink during the day, for breakfast, lunch, dinner, and snacks?
- Who does the cooking? Who does the grocery shopping? Where's the grocery store? What's in the refrigerator? What's in the cupboards?
- Are they taking showers? Baths? Washing up? Brushing their teeth? Brushing their hair?
- How are their clothes? Clean? Old? Don't fit? Shoes? Who does the clothes washing?
- What's the state of the house? General cleanliness inside? General state of repair? Faucets dripping? Floor clean? Windows? Clutter?
- What's the state of the exterior of the house? Lawn? Roof? Siding? Garage?
- What's their schedule like? Medical appointments? Hair? Social gatherings? Church?
- Do they have any hobbies? Are there requirements for their hobbies?
- What is the state and age of the cars? What are their transportation options?

How do they go about accomplishing what they choose to do or have to do? How easy is it for them to go and do it? All of these things change over time. My mother used to golf, and she loved it. She was at the golf course three days a week playing with her sister, and she was also in a league. She had such a good time. Then, she started to get lost and stopped going. One of her outlets that was so good for her (and my dad) was gone. Her world had just gotten smaller. How small has your parents' world become?

Most items fall into the following categories:

1. nutrition
2. personal cleanliness
3. environmental cleanliness (house and yard)
4. social activities and getting around

Let's take each one in order, and

- identify what you need to be aware of;
- make suggestions of what you may be able to do; and
- figure out what external help may be out there as the situation evolves.

Nutrition

As the ability or desire to prepare their own meals decreases, nutrition may take a backseat. Also, their sense of taste changes or the medication they take may alter their taste buds. Maybe not much tastes good anymore. A body that's changing or running out of steam needs significant, good nutrition to keep as active as possible. It also means feeling as good as possible. That means purchasing and preparing food. I worked with an elderly woman who had a collection of cookbooks, a whole bookshelf full. It filled one wall in her dining area. Well, she wasn't cooking anymore, and in her refrigerator and cupboards were a lot of processed foods, frozen dinners, and the like. She had no desire to cook, and she was slightly disabled and couldn't stand for any length of time. So this cook wasn't cooking. She did receive Meals on Wheels, so she had a nutritious and well-balanced meal once a day. Both my parents and my in-laws went to a Meals on Wheels program. But we had a struggle to get them to agree to accept it. It's an admission that they cannot handle this part of life anymore, and it's hard to accept.

So here are some things you might try to do to help. Observe first. Figure out what you can do to help second. Enlist outside help third.

Always check what's in the refrigerator and the cupboards. How old is the food? We checked the refrigerator every time we went to the parents' house. We found partially eaten cans of soup, the meal that we brought over on our last visit, or the leftovers from the deli and ground beef stored in the underwear drawer (dementia related). Throw out what's bad or potentially bad. It helped us understand what they were eating.

Part of nutrition is hydration. Drinking water or other liquids throughout the day is critical to making someone feel better. My father had congestive heart failure, so it was very important for him to drink liquids. We were called home several times because he thought he was dying when all that was wrong was that he was dehydrated. But there was another side to this. He was weak and struggled just to get up. So going to the bathroom was difficult because of his hampered movement. His decision then was not to drink much. Then he wouldn't have to go to the bathroom. During the night, he used a plastic urinal that was placed next to his bed. He used it at night, but he refused to have it next to his chair in the living room during the day.

Conflicting needs coupled with physical limitations make for a challenge, and there isn't much you can do about that. My father's struggles to stand up were painful to watch, but his philosophy was the struggle was worth it. If he didn't struggle to stand up and move, then he was doomed to live out his life in a wheelchair. He said, "Once I get in one of those things [meaning a wheelchair], I'll never get out." He was right. One item we purchased (and Medicare *may* pay for part of it) was a lift chair. It looks like a recliner and has a motor on it that raises the chair seat for easier sitting down or getting up. My father used that daily. This type of assistance is readily available and worth purchasing. It helps the person get into the chair and out of the chair, and it looks like a regular recliner.

In terms of food, if they still can cook and want to but getting to the grocery store is difficult, there might be a delivery service or the ability to order food items over the Internet. That option might be available where you live. There are also prepared or semi-prepared meals through some businesses. Order a set of meals for the week, and they come ready with minimal preparation. That might be another option. Meals on Wheels programs are run in communities by any number of organizations. Sometimes a church or the visiting nurse association will take on that responsibility. Volunteers drive the meals on a daily basis to those who have ordered them.

Some programs are available seven days a week; others only five days a week. Your local area social services department would know whom to contact for that service. We fought both sets of parents on this topic but eventually prevailed. The technique I used with my father-in-law was first, I did the research. Second, I sat down with him and just asked which Meals on Wheels service he would like. I never asked him if he wanted it; I just asked him which one he was choosing.

With Meals on Wheels, which is paid for by the person ordering (the meals are subsidized), someone is walking into the elder's house every day. This can be a blessing and a comfort. Consider it another pair of eyes on the situation. They don't stay long, but they get to know the individuals and are another witness to the situation. I know for my folks' situation, the Meals on Wheels folks were required to report any neglect or abuse that they may witness to the local social services. I do not know if that is typical or widespread. I hope so.

Here are some ideas for what you can do:

- Prepare meals at your home, and bring them to your parents.
- Do the cooking when you're there, and have plenty for leftovers.
- Go grocery shopping for staples to make sure they can make a sandwich or heat a can of soup.
- Do the dishes.
- Clean the countertops, stove tops, and refrigerator.
- Unplug the stove if you are concerned about fire.
- Do the research for what food delivery and food preparation there is in that locality.
- If there is a senior center and they are willing to go, find out when meals are served and take them there. Socialization plus food is a good mix.
- Research local grocery stores and see if they have a delivery service.
- Bake them a cake.

Some outside groups can help:

- local senior center
- local senior resource centers—locate food services

- local church outreach
- Meals on Wheels program

Personal Cleanliness

Do they shower? Do they brush their teeth? When was the last time they went to the dentist? Do they wash their clothes? Do they recognize dirty clothes or a dirty face? What's the layout of the bathrooms? Is it a low or high toilet? Are there grab bars next to the toilet or in the shower/bathtub? Do they stink?

When visiting my father-in-law in the hospital for a hip replacement, I was sitting next to my mother-in-law. She stank. I told my husband, and he diplomatically asked his mother when she last showered. What we then found out was she was staying in the room with her husband and the shower in the room didn't work. She was afraid to drive home and then drive back to the hospital. When his meals were brought in, they split the meal. It was one of those wake-up calls you get just observing what's happening and saying something, rather than just ignoring the situation. So my husband fixed the shower in the hospital room, and his mother started showering again.

In another example, the son fixed the shower stall at his parents' cottage. The parents typically stayed out at their cottage all summer with weekly trips back to their main house to do laundry, check on mail, and so on. Well, two months after the son fixed the shower stall, he asked how it was working. The parents didn't know. They hadn't used it. They probably showered at home during one of their weekly trips; however, at the cottage, they weren't showering. You know your heart sinks when you hear something like that, and there isn't much you can do. Just make sure that all items like showers are in good working condition.

We eventually hired a home health nurse to come in and help my father get ready in the morning. She came two or three times a week. Yes, my parents paid for that, but it was worth it. We also had a shower chair in the tub so my father and mother could sit down while taking a shower. There was a grab bar. And we changed out the toilet to a higher model and put a grab bar on the wall next to it. You can visit a home health store and get ideas from them as to what products and installers are available.

If you are staying with them, try to witness when they do wash or shower. We would observe my mother going into the bathroom at about 4:00 p.m. (her usual shower time). However, after dementia settled in, she would not shower. The shower had become too much of a task for her, yet she still went into the bathroom. Maybe she ran water; we weren't sure. For someone with dementia, taking a shower is a deluge of decisions resulting in overload for the person.

Neither set of parents washed clothes toward the end of their lives at home. Sometimes my mother-in-law would wash one item, but she no longer had any concept of clothes washing. Nor did my mother, who eventually couldn't run the washing machine. So we did it. Well, we would check to see if there were any dirty clothes, and in both cases, there were no dirty clothes in the baskets, meaning, they weren't changing their clothes. My sister would set out clean clothes for them and do laundry when she was there. That way, my parents did change clothes. But left to themselves, they were no changes of clothes. At my in-laws', we cleaned out their closets so it was more obvious which clothing was available, clean, and wearable. And I washed everything else.

Do they go to the dentist? Yes it might be hard to get there, but take a day off of work and drive them to appointments. That was what we did. Get them to see the professionals. It was a dentist who noticed the tumor in my father-in-law's mouth. It was that dentist who got him analyzed and tested and found the cancer—a dentist.

Ideas for you:

- Have safety items (grab bar, shower chair, high toilet) installed.
- Possibly remodel the bathroom to have a walk-in shower or wider doorway.
- When you visit, clean the bathrooms.
- Do the laundry.
- Organize closets.
- Research local in-home health aid groups to help with a morning routine.

For outside help:

1. Interview and visit in-home health groups.
2. Hire someone to help with personal cleanliness.

3. Talk to someone who remodels and has experience with elderly people. You might talk to an assisted living place or visit one to see how they set up their bathrooms.

Environmental Cleanliness

What does the home look like? Is anyone doing cleaning? For my in-laws, they hired a person to do light housekeeping and chores. For my parents, whenever we were there (and that was multiple times during the week), we all took time to do house-keeping. Get a work crew together, and do spring housecleaning or have monthly yardwork get-togethers. However you can configure it, they will need help with the house and the yard.

Mow the lawn, weed the garden, plant flowers, and wash windows. Sometimes I felt that I did more at the parents' home than I did at mine. Sometimes that was true. Check with the local senior resource center or a group called RSVP. They sometimes run a program that helps the elderly with transportation and with home chores. Our neighbor was connected with the area's elder group, and he had a volunteer help with mowing the lawn and shoveling snow. A church outreach program may also do that type of work. Is there a neighborhood kid who would like to earn some money?

If you do an Internet search for "senior resources," you will come up with a lot of different names for similar types of organizations, all centered around providing services for the elderly. Attach the state that you are in to that query and you will find your regional services.

A house takes maintenance. Check around and see what needs to be done. Does the furnace work? Are there leaks in the basement? Does the outside trim need mainte-nance? You'll have to figure out a way to get those items accomplished.

Take out their garbage. Do they have to take their garbage to the curb? Is that easily done? One city provided a service for the elderly by arranging for the sanitation workers to come up to the house rather than having the elderly folks walk their garbage cans to the curb. Check and see if your municipality does that. That is a nice service.

Things you can do:

- Mow the lawn and weed-whack.
- Wash windows on the outside, and if they still use storm windows, put them up or take them down.
- Trim bushes, sweep sidewalks, and paint the trim (or hire someone to do that).
- Clean gutters, or shovel snow off of the garage roof because it's too weighty. (I did that one winter weekend).
- Check that the heat and plumbing work. Have the furnace checked out once a year.
- Just do or hire someone to do whatever you would do at your own home.

For outside help:

- RSVP or local senior centers have volunteers that will do some chores.
- Is there a local handyman available for jobs you need to hire out?
- Do they have a church affiliation? Sometimes churches have outreach programs.

Social Activities

What activities are your parents involved with or used to be? Is there a reason they stopped? Is it because of transportation or an inability to do the activity? Transportation is an extremely difficult problem to solve. A group called RSVP may have transportation options available, giving people rides where they need to go. A friend of mine volunteered to provide rides through RSVP. The elder would call RSVP and ask for a ride (they needed a twenty-four-hour notice), and RSVP would go down their list of volunteers and assign someone the driving task. RSVP is a national volunteer organization.

Also, if possible, the city's bus system may provide assistance for the elderly. Where I lived, the city bus representative would come to your house and help you get to the bus stop, ride the bus with you, get off with you, and teach you how to use the city's public transportation. They would help you learn which routes to take. One issue is that you still have to get to the bus stop. However, depending on your location and capability, this might be an option.

Relying on friends, the neighborhood senior center volunteers, or family may be your only option. For localized neighborhood travel, sometimes a scooter works well. It can get someone around his or her yard or down the block. Golf carts are also an option for closer destinations. In elderly housing, many times, the housing managers organize shopping trips, Sunday church service trips, or other recreational opportunities. They may charge a modest fee, or it may be free if you live in the housing.

Are they bored? Did you ever think about that? If it takes you until noon to wake up and have a piece of toast, would you be bored? Are you bored? Are you bored with caregiving activities or with your visits, or are you bored with the situation? Whom do your parents talk to during the day? What do they do? Where do they go? What is the level and nature of their interactions? How bored would you be if the only people you talked to were the grocery store clerks, the pharmacist, and the doctor?

Many elderly people are bored. And it's because they can't get around and don't know how to solve the problem or they can't hear well. So they stay inside their house, and their world shrinks. Possibly their hearing is compromised, and in groups, even small groups, they just don't hear well. Or they are embarrassed. They don't want to be seen looking the way they do. They may be embarrassed about their disability, wheelchair, dementia, cane, or walker.

The more they engage, the better they will be. When they see a purpose and the next project, they still feel alive. Sometimes when they move out of their own house and into housing for the elderly or assisted living, they become healthier and happier. There are people around and options for their living within senior housing. Many facilities organize trips, card games, gardening, or handyman types of activities. These support the elders' feelings of worth. They still want to feel that they are worth it.

Maybe their social activities have to change a bit. Many senior centers offer a wide variety of activities. Some school systems have a program for adopting a grandparent. Youth and vitality positively affect older adults. The most difficult part of continuing to engage in social activities is often transportation.

What kind of help can you provide? If you are long-distance, not much. But can you research the help that's available in the area? Can you find some local volunteer group where your parents live to see if transportation or chores or companionship is offered? Be there during their first encounter with these folks, if at all possible. You always want to know who is coming into your parents' home.

Maybe you have to come up with projects for them to do. Have you got that family history recorded? Are the people in the pictures identified? Is technology part of the solution? Facebook?

One of the issues with help is what it costs. Outline what the costs are so that they know. Find out if they can afford it. If they aren't driving anymore, does the cost of owning and maintaining a car offset the cost of help? Does paying for Meals on Wheels offset the cost of pizza deliveries or wasted food from the grocery store? Why do your parents have difficulty getting around? What's the cause? Think about it.

As an example, if your parent has difficulty standing up, why?

1. Did he or she have a stroke and lose upper body strength, or is he or she in a generally weakened condition?
2. Does your parent suffer from vertigo, or is he or she shaky?
3. Does he or she have dementia? Can he or she figure out how to get from sitting to standing?
4. Is there a fear of falling?
5. Does he or she have bad feet, knees, or hips so the movement is restricted?
6. Is he or she bored or depressed? Does he or she have a reason to get up?

If you can identify the reason you have a better chance of identifying what help would be appropriate. Your parent needs help and may not know how to ask for it, may not want to ask for it, or may be unaware that the help he or she needs exists. Your parent may also be worried about how much help costs, and depending on the reason, there may be no way to help, but maybe there's a way to make things safer.

Through normal, everyday activities, accidents happen. This is where the crises occur (other than health crises)—the falls, the burning dinner, the furnace or electric going out, or tripping on outside hazards. Modifying the home to accommodate some of these concerns may be an option. I talked with a business that had equipment and did modifications in homes for the elderly. I was shown a lift system that could be installed so that the individual could lift him-or herself into a harness and get to the bathroom, all by him- or herself, even though the individual couldn't walk. This lift system costs about fifteen thousand dollars, but it might allow someone to remain in his or her home for another year or so. Fifteen thousand dollars would last about 2.2 months in a nursing home. Investing in some modifications could help an individual retain some independence and be safer and keep him or her home for a little while longer.

Sometimes you can convince elders that giving up their pride and accepting some help might give them more independence in the short term. As an example, we fought with one tough old World War II veteran to have a ramp built. He didn't want any stupid, invalid-indicating ramp out his front door. But we rammed it through. He then got a scooter. He could barely walk anymore and hadn't been out of his house on his own in a couple of years. With the ramp and scooter, he left his house for the first time on his own, with no one helping him or carrying him. Independence. He could get out of the house when he wanted to, and then he could wander around his yard and get back into the house on his terms, not someone else's. This is independence. Getting people to see that this thing, whatever it is, could help them is difficult and sometimes impossible. And yet their lives would improve a little bit anyway.

The normal living activities are difficult. There are so many things that you don't even think about because they are so natural. When they don't occur naturally, you're amazed, puzzled, stumped, frustrated, and sometimes, helpless.

On Helplessness

Definition (from *Merriam-Webster On-Line Dictionary*)

> *Helpless:* (adjective, Helplessness-noun)
> Not protected: not able to defend yourself unable to do something to
> make a situation, task, etc., better or easier not able to be controlled

Helplessness is the feeling of not being able to do anything or not doing anything that would help a situation or a person. You feel useless. You feel as if nothing you do will change the situation to a positive.

Caring for elderly people has helplessness as part of the process because, in many cases, there isn't anything you can do. Or nothing that you do is going to relieve the situation. Maybe what you do only ensures their safety or that they have good food. But what you do is not going to improve or fix anything or create a wonderful situation. You do need to learn to live with this feeling. Just think how helpless your parents are feeling.

In this section, I present to you a situation that we went through. It is somewhat dramatic and demonstrates starkly the helplessness that is very real. There was nothing we could do about it. As I said in the introduction (please read it if you skipped it), all examples and situations I place in this book are real. They either happened to us or people I worked with. This happened to us.

I was at work in midafternoon on a very normal day. My husband was also at work. My phone rang.

Here is my side of the phone call:

> "Hello, this is Janine." I recognized the phone exchange from my
> husband's work, but it wasn't his number. Immediate concern.
> "Hmmm!"
> "Oh no!"

"What @?#?"
"Oh my God!"
"Yes."
"Okay."
"Right away."
"Okay"
"Bye."

Do you feel helpless? Do you know what to do? Do you know how to handle this situation? Is there anything you can do? Was there anything you could have done to prevent this situation?

Of course, you don't have the other part to the conversation. It'll add drama, and you'll understand my responses, but there was nothing else to do. Helpless. There was nothing we could have done to prevent this situation. We just had to live with it and deal with it.

After this phone call, I did what I was asked to do and then I sat back at my desk and just sat there, thinking, wondering, worrying, not working. In the scheme of things, work was reduced to meaningless trivia. It seemed like such a waste of time. There was nothing significant or worthwhile to accomplish there. Work.

I waited for my husband to call back, but I knew that it was possible I would have to wait until I got home—two hours from then. The following is the full conversation.

Phone rings:

Me: "Hello, this is Janine."
Husband: "I'm calling from the phone next to me. I'm on my phone with my mother and the nine-one-one center."
Me: "Hmmm?"
Husband: "I may have to hang up soon, but Mom called me here at work. Dad has threatened to kill himself so I had her call nine-one-one. I'm on the line with both of them right now."

Me: "Oh no!"

Husband: "They are sending the SWAT team over to the house."

Me: "*What*! @?#?"

Husband: "I told them that yes there was a gun in the house and told them of the current situation with the folks."

Me: "Oh my God!"

Husband: "Can you call John and let him know what is going on and that the SWAT team will be there surrounding the house soon."

Me: "Yes."

Husband: "Pat is on his way to the folks'."

Me: "Okay."

Husband: "Call John."

Me: "Right away.'

Husband: "I gotta go."

Me: "Okay."

Husband: "Bye—talk to you later. Might not call back before I go home."

Me: "Bye."

Helpless. We're ninety miles away. Pat is fifty miles away. Pat is my husband's brother. The nine-one-one operator had patched my husband into the phone conversation with his mom. How she was able to call my husband at work remains a mystery.

I called John and let him know what the situation was. He was a good neighbor and appreciated the heads-up. I asked him to call the other neighbors to let them know. I also told him that Pat was on the way.

So I imagined what it would look like at my in-laws' house. They were such decent, law-abiding, hardworking normal people. The *SWAT* team? My goodness. What triggered my mother-in-law to call? Was it that serious of a threat? Things were not going my father-in-law's way; that was for sure. But was he serious? Did he have a gun out? Had he just had enough? He was dying of three different kinds of cancer, and his wife had mid-stage dementia. Everything was a chore and hard, and nothing was getting easier. Every day was ugly, and there was not going to be any relief.

I left work as early as would be appropriate and raced home. My husband was there. I asked if he wanted to drive to his folks, and he said, "No." That surprised me. But I think he felt that we would make matters worse. My father-in-law would be mortified.

Later, after my brother-in-law called, we found out that the police department had sent a woman to handle the conversation with my father-in-law. She seemed trained in conversations with the elderly. She diffused the situation well and professionally. My father-in-law had not retrieved any of his guns. He told the police where his handgun was, and it was so secure that my father-in-law in his weakened condition wouldn't have been able to retrieve it. The police gave it to my brother-in-law, who then took it back to his house.

My brother-in-law then drove back to his house, and we sat. I cannot imagine what was going through my father-in-law's mind and heart at the end of this day.

Helpless. Both him and us. There was nothing that we could do. We were helpless.

CHAPTER 4
Finances

This chapter covers a lot of information. Financial and legal information are tied so closely that many items will be mentioned in both chapter 4 and chapter 5 "Legal Information." In both chapters, all numbers given are approximations. Your geographic area will have different parameters. Your state will have different rules. Please assume that the numbers are meant as a benchmark so that you know the range of the money involved. As an example, if I state that something costs $500, know that for you, it may be $400 or $750.49. I don't know for sure what it will cost you, but the numbers will give you an idea. I hope these numbers will help you prepare and plan for the expenses that will come. I also hope the information will prevent you from making a significant monetary mistake.

The first part of this chapter is about how to discover what the finances of your parents are. We talk about their income and their expenses as well as their assets (assets are what they own and have) and their liabilities (what they owe). Next we cover some financial options that are available. Not all options may be available in your area, and not all options will work for your situation. Being aware of their existence may help you identify your plan of action. I'll also mention people in your community who can help.

The biggest questions for you are: How can you plan without knowing the numbers? How can you pay bills or plan how to allocate their money without knowing what it is?

You must learn as much as you can about your parents' financial situation. You need to understand what all of their assets are and what all their liabilities are. There are so many ways to make sure your parents are well cared for, now and in the future, and using their money wisely is key.

But to use the money wisely, you need to know how much there is. Depending upon your situation, there are financial planners who specialize in the last phase of life planning. This isn't retirement planning. This is about how your parents get taken care of for the rest of their days with their financial situation the way it is. Most of the time, it's the people with modest incomes who need the most planning help. If there is such a planner in your area, it may be worth it to talk to him or her. These planners know the ins and outs of financial setups that may leverage your parents' assets most effectively. It's a resource available to you, and you may need that type of help. Just like with attorneys, however, if you are not comfortable with the individual, do not do business with him or her.

With or without financial planning help, you need to know what your parents have, so write down what you know.

Assets (what they have and own):

1. house (last market value or appraisal)
2. checking and savings accounts, safety deposit box
3. retirement accounts, IRAs, pensions
4. brokerage accounts/financial plans
5. whole life insurance or term life insurance
6. long-term-care insurance (I include this as an asset even though it is a monthly expense because it converts to monthly income when accessed)
7. house contents (anything special like artwork, jewelry, collections)
8. prepaid funeral
9. cars, vehicles, and boats
10. other land, cottages, cabins, or acreage somewhere
11. CDs, bonds, money in shoeboxes

Don't forget to look under the mattress.

Money is one of the huge constraints of caregiving—that and time. Money will determine how much outside help you can hire and whether your parents can afford a facility. Look at their bank statements, and find out what the balance is each month. That amount may be what can be used to help them afford in-home help. They may have assets that they can leverage, like their home (either a home equity loan or a reverse mortgage), whole life insurance (it may be able to be turned into a monthly annuity or cashed out), or physical assets (land, cottage, boat, and so on), and cash in those CDs. I'm not recommending that any of these are appropriate for your situation. However, each is an option to consider. One or more of them may fit and be a good option for you. Talking with a financial planner may be the best way to find out if any of these are a good alternative. Your parents may have more money available to them than you originally thought.

Note: This isn't about you getting to invest or spend their money. It's about how to use their own money effectively to take care of them in the best way possible. It's not your money.

So now list their income:

1. Social Security
2. pensions (including veteran's benefits)
3. annuities, IRAs
4. outside income (rental, work-related)
5. interest

Can their income sustain them and for how long in the following situations:

- in their own home with in-home help
- in a facility for a certain amount of time

If they sell their house, how long will that money last?

You don't have to do this all at once. One way to find out their overall financial situation is to do their taxes. This gives a very good picture of their financial situation for an annual view. At least review their taxes. Look at their bank statements. Bank statements help you with a monthly overview of their finances. If you can get online access to their accounts, you can keep daily track of the accounts. Through the bank statements or online accounts, you can see the income and the expenses. When does the income come in? When are the expenses going out? What is automatic? What could be automatic? Over a couple of months, you can determine the normal expenses and incomes. Do not forget about periodic payments, including the quarterly or annual expenses, such as insurance and taxes.

In chapter 2, "Health," you gathered the costs for their current health care. Here are those numbers again from chapter 2. Know that regional differences exist. These numbers are here to give you an idea of what the costs are, not to tell you what things will cost.

Some numbers to help you (in 2014 Midwest dollars)

1. in their own home with in-home help: $25 to $35 per hour, usually with a three-hour minimum depending on the level of help
2. independent living apartments or condos: $800 per month rent; for condos, whatever the market is bearing—usually over $100,000 purchase price
3. assisted living: approximately $3,500 per month
4. group home: $5,500 per month
5. memory care center: $6,000 per month
6. nursing home: $6,800 per month

Liabilities (what they owe)

1. rent, mortgage, or condo fees
2. real estate taxes, income taxes, and local taxes
3. insurance costs (house, renter's, liability, long-term care)
4. house maintenance (lawn care, house cleaning)
5. utilities
6. doctor's bills (dentist, eye, medical)
7. food, entertainment
8. vehicle costs
9. loans

Looking at their bank statements will help with monthly expenses but may not indicate some of the annual expenditures, such as real estate taxes and house and car insurance. So if there are other than monthly expenses, you will have to find out what those are. If you like spreadsheets, you may want to set one up and track what's happening. Many online bank services allow you to export the transactions into a file readable by a spreadsheet.

How can you manage their funds without access to them?

- Do you know where the key is to the safety deposit box? At what bank or credit union is the safety deposit box?
- Do you know their IDs and passwords to any online accounts?
- Do you know who their financial planner is (if they have one)?
- Do you know who their insurance agent is?
- If they have brokerage accounts, what and where are they and how do you access them?

Getting access to their information may not be a smooth road. It may require one of the documents we talk about later, like a durable financial power of attorney or at least a power of attorney. Your parents may allow you to get online access with whatever their IDs and passwords are for the accounts without a formal document. Another document or legal procedure you may have to go through is the assignment of a representative payee. That would be you or the person chosen by the parents or the family. That individual will be managing the Social Security money. The representative payee only manages Social Security dollars. (More about this in chapter 5, "Legal Information").

We were lucky with our parents. My father sat us each down and explained what their financial situation was. He told us where all the documents were. My sister did their taxes for them, so she was right on top of it. My in-laws were a very different circumstance.

I started gathering financial information about my in-laws by sneaking behind my father-in-law's back and looking at bank statements and overdue real estate tax notices. That was how I got started. Every time we saw them (multiple times a week), I looked through their mail. My father-in-law didn't share any information, so that was the only way I could start to understand what their finances were.

Then I helped him with his taxes one year. He griped a lot, but I ignored it. I saw what his pension and Social Security were. I found out that they had an okay amount of monthly income. They could afford some help on a weekly basis. However, we would have to sell their house if either one or both went into a facility. They also were carrying at least $7,000 in their checking account. There wasn't much in their savings account, and they also had a CD at a savings and loan organization. They had a little bit in a brokerage account. The other asset that they had was a cottage and the associated land. That also would have to be sold to support them. Their ready cash or easily convertible to cash wasn't enough to support them in a facility. But their cash and income was enough to have some in-home help. Going through their finances a piece at a time showed us what we were going to have to do when and if the time came for them to go to a facility.

Note: It is not your responsibility to pay for your parents' bills. You can always choose to do that if you feel that is something you want to do and you can afford to do it. None of us were ever in that situation to pay for our parents' needs.

If at all possible, call the insurance agents and the financial planner or brokerage agent and introduce yourself. Set up a meeting with them to talk about the current situation and see if they have suggestions. Include your parents in the conversations if possible. Do not do this behind their backs. No one is trying to steal or fritter away their money. But you, as the caregiver, need to understand how to pay their bills now and in the future. And you need to tell your parents how you plan to proceed. Another thing that we did was go to the bank that my in-laws used and introduced ourselves. We wanted the neighborhood bank to know who we were and that we were going to be helping my in-laws. We had the durable power of attorney in place to be able to do that. Chapter 5 defines what this is. You will need the durable power of attorney to close out any brokerage accounts or financial services accounts. This may be more difficult than you anticipate, but if you have met with the agent for the financial services company, leverage him or her to help with his or her own company's customer service representatives. The money in these accounts was saved by your parents for their own care. If it is time to use the money, then you need to understand how to get it and how to leverage it.

Did you know that at the death of one of a couple, the survivor *may* receive an increase in his or her Social Security amount? When my father died (and he received more Social Security than my mother), my mother's Social Security was increased then to match what my father had received. So the one with the lower Social Security begins to receive the higher amount. Also at the death of a spouse, there is a one-time payment of $255 sent to the survivor. Its original intent was to help cover expenses upon the death of an individual. This amount also changes over time. Also know, depending upon when Social Security monthly payment is received, that when the person dies, you may have to send back that one month's Social Security.

Financial Resources

When reviewing your parents' financial situation, know that there is help out there in your community. Your city's or state's official website may outline some help. Here is a laundry list of some help to consider:

- Medicaid—This is a joint state and federal program that can help pay for nursing home costs and medical costs for the elderly. There are strict income requirements for qualifications. If your parents don't have enough assets or income, they may qualify for Medicaid. When they run out of money that obviously is the time when they will qualify for Medicaid. My mother eventually went on Medicaid at age eighty-eight. Her whole life she paid her own way and even for the first year of her nursing home stay. Then, she just ran out of money and went on Medicaid. She had no pensions, just Social Security. The majority of the Social Security went toward the nursing home cost. Medicaid needs to be planned for. You will have to work with a city, county, or state social worker to plan this out. It requires a great deal of documentation and paperwork. It is good to start ahead of time.

  Facilities need to know that an individual is going onto Medicaid, since the process takes time, but they will get paid by Medicaid eventually. This may take over a month or two to get it set up. Work with the facility to ensure that your parent stays there. Most facilities are willing and able to do this. They understand the issues regarding Medicaid.

- Rental assistance and utility assistance or food stamps—These programs all do similar things. If your parents qualify, these programs subsidize the cost of those items. If your parents live in a rental community, you need to check with the building to find out whether the property is in a subsidized program. It really can mean a lot to the parent. Many local utilities run subsidized programs for people with limited incomes. It keeps the heat and lights on. Usually to get into these programs, your parents will have to be associated with a city, county, or state social worker. You can call your local aging resource center (called all sorts of things), and find out how these processes work. In one case that I worked on, I got the elderly woman's social worker to apply for rental assistance, and it took this woman's rent down $180. That was another $180 a month that she had available to her, and she needed it. Rental subsidies can help out a lot. For some of you, $180 may not seem like a lot of money. When you are on the brink of disaster, $180 can be a lifeline. Don't turn your nose up at this help. It's there for a reason, and your parents may need this type of help. This isn't about your ego; it is about helping out your parents and utilizing these services and options that were put in place for exactly the circumstances you face.

- For veterans and their spouses, Aid and Attendance is a pension given to certain veterans depending upon their service during a designated wartime period. This benefit is also tied to finances, but much latitude is given. Aid and Attendance can be used to help pay for in-home help and may also be applied toward the cost of facilities. Check with the VA or your county's veteran representative for the qualifications. It's worth checking into. Many veterans and their spouses have been helped with this program. Personally, I helped one couple increase their monthly income by close to $1,000 per month, which helped them pay for the in-home help that they so desperately needed. It helped them stay in their home and relieved the pressure of running out of money. Veterans are worth it. Take the time to check it out.

- Local community programs—There may be localized programs set up to help the elderly stay in their homes. It could be subsidized transportation, a stipend to pay for in-home help, or local outreach programs. Each city, county, and state is different. Depending on the area, there may be a very long waiting list. But it's worth a try. Your local senior resources center can help you find out about these programs. Your parents' church may also offer outreach programs. You need to research this.

- Your parents' assets—Can the house be used to get a reverse mortgage or a home equity loan? In some cases, these may be options for your parents. With a reverse mortgage, the parent has to live in the home, and the house has to be paid for. The reverse mortgage becomes a monthly (or lump sum) payment to the home owner. This can help with in-home help or modifying the home for disability access. You need to be careful entering into a reverse mortgage and make sure you understand its limitations and weaknesses and its costs. It is a mortgage so there are closing costs. As soon as the parent moves out, the reverse mortgage comes due. It does have to be paid back and will be paid back with the sale of the house. But in some cases, this may be a good option. Other items that are parents' assets, like whole life insurance, may also be turned into a monthly annuity or a lump sum payment. Again, just be careful.

- If your parents have insurance, what kind is it? Term or whole life? Term insurance typically is used to cover the final expenses—in other words, the cost of the funeral. Funeral costs are in the eight-thousand-dollar range. Whole life insurance is different and may be cashed out to help with current monthly costs. Depending on its face value, it too can be used for the funeral costs. When and if you call a life insurance company, typically the first customer service representatives may not know their company's products well enough to answer correctly. Dig deeper into the company, and get a manager if you are not satisfied with the answer. You need to validate what the first person has said. Your parents' insurance policy may not help them with current expenses, but it's worth asking about. We had one representative tell us the wrong thing, and when I quoted their own product literature to her, she didn't know what I was talking about. So I asked for a manager. The customer service representative was wrong. I had the literature, and I had read it. Be prepared for these conversations.

Have you ever read your own insurance documents? It might be helpful. With all of these options, you need to be prepared for the conversations. Reading insurance documentation may be a yawner, but it could be the sort of leverage that helps your parents. It's worth it.

This is where a good financial planner or end-of-life planner comes in very handy. These people know well what these options are and whether your situation warrants them.

Another resource that may be in your community is a daily money manager. These people specialize in managing people's money on a daily basis, making sure that the bills are paid and the checking account has enough money in it. If you are not good at managing money or you don't have the time, hire this type of person. Make sure you properly vet the individual. You must trust him or her. A friend of mine hired a daily money manager for her mother. What a relief it gave her. She lived over a thousand miles from her mother and could not manage the daily money. This manager saved her a great deal of stress and gave her peace of mind that her mother's checking account was solvent and her bills were being paid.

Financial Summary

You need to delve into your parents' financial world. What do they have, and how long will it last? This is about taking care of them wherever that may be and finding the best financial solutions to meet their needs. You need to gather the information, however hard that may be, and keep track of what their expenses are and how they will evolve. You need to understand how to leverage whatever assets they have and plan to convert those assets into cash for their help. You need to understand what the possibilities for future costs are (e.g., nursing home expenses). So you need to get started on the discovery as soon as possible. In order to do this, some legalities need to be in place.

To-Dos:

1. Find out your parents' income.
2. Find out your parents' expenses.
3. Do or review their taxes.
4. Identify their assets and their liabilities.
5. Research community help, both professional help and resources from local, county, state, and federal governments. Contact your local area aging center (or aging resource center).

CHAPTER 5
Legal Information

Note: I am not giving legal advice. I do strongly suggest, depending on your situation, that you seek legal advice. It can save your parents lots of money, stress, and unnecessary crises. If you find a good lawyer who specializes in elder law, you have found a gold mine. It's worth their fees to get your parents situated properly.

This chapter is about you having enough background to talk to a good elder law attorney or estate-planning lawyer. Not all of you will need a lawyer, but the information here may help you determine that. A good estate planning or elder law attorney can be quite helpful and save you a lot of grief. This chapter is about information that you need to know so you can get the right help that you need. It's about preparing yourself to talk to a lawyer regarding your parents' situation and to ask good, intelligent questions to both get the most out of any legal representation and minimize the cost of a lawyer. If you are aware of some things, if you know or recognize terms, and if you have acquired the right documentation, then your conversations with lawyers will be very productive and useful for your situation. It is also about what happens if you don't prepare. Not all items need a lawyer, require a lawyer, or cost you money. At least research the items listed and decide for yourself whether you need to see a lawyer, based on your family's situation.

I worked with one woman starting on this journey. We met and discussed her situation. We came up with a list of questions in preparation for her meeting her parents' lawyer. It was so useful. I documented the questions so she wouldn't forget anything, and she was able to take that list to the lawyer, conduct a very productive meeting, and get exactly what she needed for her situation. She felt good regarding that meeting and its results. It's worth your time to prepare.

This chapter will cover the following basic information about certain legal documents that are helpful and can spare you other costly options. I'll explain what their purpose is. You may not need everything, but you will need most of them. This chapter also covers the probate process which may be unfamiliar to most of us.

Legal Documents that You Need

- will
- durable power of attorney
- representative payee (possible)
- living revocable trust (optional, depends on your situation)

Will

A will is a document that outlines how you want your estate to be disbursed upon your death. Each individual should have a will. It can be very simple, and most state health and human services websites have an outline for a simple will. Check your state's official website. All the documents needed may be listed under "Advanced Directives." All of these will be free to you to download. But you *must* follow the directions.

A will contains directions as to the disbursement of the estate after the death of an individual and names the executor of the estate. The executor does not have to be a family member. It should be someone who will be honest and effective in the processing of the will. The executor is not necessarily the same person who holds either the health or the financial power of attorney. The executor of the will manages the probate process. During the probate process, the executor will be officially named. If there is a problem with the designation, others can apply and a judge will decide who is most appropriate.

The will is probated. Probate is a legal process by which the state (wherever you live) reviews the will, judges its validity, and processes the will. It typically requires an attorney to probate the will because of the applications, estate inventory, scheduling of a variety of items, and tracking and paying of all appropriate fees.

Probate costs money, and the costs are all over the map. In the Midwest, probate costs run between 1 and 7 percent of the total value of the estate. Most wills take a minimum of six months to process. In one Midwest state that is considered a state in which the probate process is quick and less expensive than other states, it still costs at a minimum 1 percent of the value of the estate and takes six months. So if 1 to 7 percent and six months is cheap and quick, you can judge for yourself what other states may be. Check your own state as to its average probate costs.

Take the total value of your parents' estate and take 3.5 percent of it. That's an approximation of the cost of probate. The probate costs will come out of the value of the estate. You will have to sell something or take money out of the estate's assets to pay the probate court and the lawyer. The time it takes can cause problems. But a quick probate is considered about six months. It takes time to do all that needs to be done. A lawyer will help keep you on track and ensure that everything is done according to the rules of your state and in a timely fashion.

The probate process is public. Anyone can request a copy of a will—anyone. If you want to, you can contact the county where Elvis died and get a copy of Elvis Presley's will. You do have to pay a modest fee for a copy. While this process doesn't make it to the evening news, the fact that probate is public may not be an issue for you. However, for other family members, know that you can follow the probate process and eventually get a copy of the will. I definitely feel very sorry for families in which there is contention over their parents' estate. We had none of that from either my parents or my in-laws. This is where greed comes into play, even if the estate is minor. I hope your family is not greedy.

The majority of assets are tied up until probate is finished. You cannot sell the house, as an example, until probate is completed. Each state is different so you must check your state's probate requirements and restrictions. Regular income and expenses may be allowed during this process. Know that when the second parent dies, the estate of the remaining spouse also goes through probate. So if the spouse inherits everything, the probate costs will occur again when the second spouse dies. In other words, the cost of probate of a couple's estate (simple wills) can almost double. Yes, there is a way around it. It's called a living revocable trust. This is discussed slightly later. You do need a lawyer to create a legal proper trust.

In some states, there may be a shortened probate process depending upon the will and value of the estate. If the will is very simple and no one contests the will, the probate costs would be minimal and the time for the probate process would also be relatively short. The probate may not require court appearances. A simple probate process may be able to be done using phones, faxes, and mail. Check your state bar association's website and your state's website to get an understanding of what to expect. An example of a simple will may be the individual wills all the assets to be divided equally among the children. Also, in some states, if the value of the estate is below a certain amount, there is no probate. It's not worth it to the state to process the will of an estate with so little value. In that case, the estate can be liquidated as soon as the state is notified as to the death of the individual and his or her estate value. This still requires some documentation.

Your state bar association may offer a description of the probate process. Check the websites of your state bar association. Also, law firms may offer free seminars on the probate process or planning for such an event. They may offer seminars on advanced directives. Attend one. Even though the seminars are all sales jobs, it is worth attending to help you understand the process and get used to the terminology that is used. I attended free seminars frequently. It gave me names of lawyers and an understanding of the terminology and processes. It was very helpful.

When considering the death of a parent, you also need to understand, in your state, whether you have *death* or *inheritance taxes*. You will have to set aside money from the estate or from your inheritance to pay those taxes. Not all states have them. At some level, the federal government has them. But you need to check for your state and the federal government. There may be limits as to when an estate incurs those taxes. As an example, if the value of the estate is less than five million dollars, there may be no death tax or, for those who inherit, no inheritance tax. Each state is different.

If the estate to be probated has property in more than one state (e.g., a cottage on a lake in a different state), both states will require a probate. So the executor of the estate will travel to both (or more) states to probate the will. Since the laws and rules are different for each state, you will want to get a lawyer to help you out. You may need a lawyer in each state that the will is probated in. Yes, the implication here is the cost of the probate will be more because more than one state is involved.

What happens if your parent doesn't have a will? In most states, the state will decide how to divide up the estate. This state-imposed will is probated. The state will do it logically (e.g., current spouse first, children second). This of course may take more time and costs money as the family is researched. It's worth having a will versus having the state decide who gets what. If your state's official website has a list of the advanced directives, download their version of a will and fill in the blanks. Follow the directions as to how it becomes valid (notary signatures or witnesses), and get one created. It saves time, money, stress, and squabbles (some of them). Take control of your own estate. Have your parents take control of their estate. Don't let someone else (the state) decide for you.

So check with your parents and make sure they have a will, they have an executor (or personal representative) named, and that person still makes sense to be the executor. Otherwise, change the executor. Also, find out where the will is. If you cannot find it, the state assumes it does not exist. If your parents do not have a will, download your free copy from the state's official website and get them to fill it in.

A will is a simple thing to create, and it either costs no money or just a little. It prevents confusion and arguments as to the person's intent. It still may cause anger or bitterness depending on the disposition of an estate. I have found during this process or discussion, greed rears its ugly head. People become greedy over some of the silliest and least valuable things. Be watchful. The person who is making the will has every right to dispose of his or her own assets whichever way he or she chooses. Maybe it seems silly or stupid or vengeful to some, and maybe it is. However, it's still that individual's own assets. We hope the executor is honest and has integrity. It makes the process work much more smoothly.

If at all concerned about creating a will, contact a lawyer to have one drawn up. It won't cost much money. It may be a flat fee and most likely under $500.

To-Dos

1. Establish if your parents have a will. Each person needs to have a will.
2. Locate the wills.
3. Find out who the executor is, and validate that the executor is still appropriate.
4. If no will, go to your state's website and find information about wills and powers of attorney. Download them. Have your parents fill them out according to what they want. Make sure they are properly witnessed (or notarized) according to the rules in your state.

Now on to the next set of documents. Just like the HCPOA, a durable power of attorney (financial power of attorney) is critical.

Durable Power of Attorney

My Definition:

> A power of attorney that will put the responsibility for someone's financial resources/responsibilities into someone else's hands. This can be highly restrictive or wide open. It transcends incapacitation. Ends at the death of the individual.

There is a difference between power of attorney (POA) and durable power of attorney (DPOA). If an individual has the regular power of attorney, that POA is suspended during incapacitation. For example, if an individual has a stroke, the regular POA would be suspended until the individual is cognizant enough to handle his or her own affairs.

Why would a person have a regular POA in effect? An individual chooses to have someone else handle his or her finances even though he or she is cognitively healthy. One possibility is that the individual lives in two different areas of the country during the year and wants someone to handle his or her bills while he or she is away. Another example of a regular POA would be someone handling the parents' financial daily activities because the person just didn't want to bother.

But if that individual becomes incompetent through a medical condition or an accident, that POA is suspended. When that individual becomes healthy enough again and able to handle his or her own affairs again, then the POA can become active again. Incapacitation may be the result of a stroke, a heart attack, or a car accident. Someone may go into a coma because of a medical condition and not be able to talk or communicate. These would be times when a regular, normal power of attorney would be suspended.

A *durable* POA gives you financial authority even if the person becomes incapacitated. Durable POA should have check-signing capability and the ability to close accounts and open them and sell a home or the contents of home. This gets critical as things progress. You need to make sure that you can cash out investments and turn them into cash in order to pay the bills. You need to make sure you can sell assets in order to pay for facility costs or pay for the in-home care or modifications to a home as needed. The financial power of attorney is not necessarily the executor of your will. The financial agent, like the health care agent, can be different from the executor of a will. The agent who is chosen obviously should be honest and trustworthy. Why would you put your assets into the hands of someone you don't trust? You wouldn't. Why would you put your assets into the hands of someone who can't manage money? You wouldn't. The person who creates the DPOA outlines within the document how it goes into effect. Just because you have one drawn up doesn't mean that it goes into effect immediately. Just like the HCPOA, it has a process to activate it.

A durable power of attorney typically, but not always, goes into effect when two doctors declare a person incapable of handling his or her affairs. This can happen because of dementia or as the result of a stroke or some other medical condition. Then the DPOA can go into effect and the agent named in the DPOA can start handling the monetary affairs.

This durable power of attorney, like the health care power of attorney, is typically available on the health and human services website of your respective state government. The generic form will list items that can be checked, and your parents select which financial powers they entrust you or their agent with. Then this document needs witnesses (or a notary) to validate the signatures. If you are the designated person to have the DPOA, then you need to carry this document with you as you work through their finances. Every financial institution will want a copy. This copy will be put on file at the various financial institutions that you will be dealing with. Carry it with you always. This document went into our briefcase that we carried around with us doing my in-laws' business. We needed it frequently.

Having the power of attorney for finances requires you to have a fiduciary responsibility. That means that you have to handle someone else's money carefully and according to his or her wishes. It does not mean that you have been given the right to do anything you want with it. If someone else sees the mishandling of finances, that person can take you to court and you will be held responsible for any wrongdoing.

Warning! We have found that many financial services companies, firms that a financial planner works for, will refuse your request to cash out the money even if you have the correct paperwork. The more money you have, the greater leverage you may have. Even with the proper paperwork, durable power of attorney, and named trustee of a trust, we have found the customer service end of financial services companies to be unhelpful. You try so hard to do everything right, you spend money to make things correct and legal, and then someone at the customer service end of the company refuses to deal with you unless you fill in their paperwork, which duplicates the paperwork that they already have. When it's our time, we do not want our designated representative to have to struggle with these issues. So we plan to convert everything to simple cash and put it in the credit union. Banks and credit unions were easy to deal with. You still need all the proper documentation and identification. Of course, you must choose what's best for you to do.

At a minimum, you, as the major caregiver, should have a durable power of attorney. You do not need to go to a lawyer to create these documents. Use the resources available to you through your state's official website. Look for "Advanced Directives." However, if you are doing more estate planning, then I highly recommend seeing a well-known estate-planning lawyer. The initial conversation with the lawyer will typically be free. You can get a sense for his or her knowledge and how comfortable you are with him or her. Many lawyers will create wills and durable powers of attorney for flat fees. However, if after any conversation you have with a lawyer, you are not comfortable with that lawyer, there are plenty more.

Do not work with someone who makes you uncomfortable!

If you do not get a DPOA, you will have to go to court to become a guardian to the parent. It is called "guardian of estate." The same situation as with the HCPOA happens. You need to get a lawyer, attend court sessions, and pay all court fees. This will cost you at least three thousand dollars. Why put yourself through this? Get the work done ahead of time and for either nothing or very little. Guardian of Estate is for financial matters and Guardian of Person is for health related issues. You can become "Guardian" for both financial and health care.

Representative Payee

A representative payee is an individual who has been named and vetted by the Social Security Administration to handle the Social Security money of one individual. You cannot do anything, including change the address of where statements from the Social Security Administration go, without being a representative payee. As long as your parents are in their home and managing their accounts, one may not be necessary. As soon as they become incapacitated and you are managing their finances, then you may need to become a representative payee. It does not matter whether you have a durable financial power of attorney. This is the government, so they require a different power and therefore different documentation. If you want to change banks to a bank in your area, you definitely have to become a representative payee.

To become a representative payee, you have to appear in person at the local Social Security office, and they ask you a series of questions. You will need to know your parents' Social Security numbers and the name and address of their doctor. They will send a form to your parents' doctor, and he or she will attest to the fact your parents are not capable of handling their finances. Each parent gets a representative payee. It takes about six weeks. You will then have to report back to the Social Security Administration on an annual basis about how you managed that money. I was a volunteer representative payee, and I created a spreadsheet to track the money. It wasn't complicated or hard, but it was easier to track on a monthly basis (rent, food, utilities, and so on) what each of those expenditures were, so that at the end of that year, I just subtotaled everything and submitted the report (online) to the Social Security Administration.

This is just another step in a long list of steps that may have to be taken. Becoming a representative payee results in you receiving all of the reports from Medicare and Medicaid (if applicable).

Living Revocable Trust

Earlier in this chapter while discussing probate, I mentioned that there is a way around the public process of probate. It's called a living revocable trust. This is not a trust that's established for the care of minor or disabled children. It is a different instrument and can be very helpful, depending upon the situation.

A living revocable trust can do many things for the finances, including describing how they should be managed. As long as the creators of the trust are the first-level trustees, they (your parents) can manage the trust the same as they manage their own assets now. They still write checks, pay bills, put money in accounts, and sell their possessions. Taxes are paid exactly the same way that they always have been paid. Nothing changes as to the ongoing management of finances or payment of taxes.

Ownership of the assets is transferred to the trust. This does two major things (there are others, but it depends on the directions in the trust).

1. It removes the estate from probate. While probate is a trusted process, it takes time and money. A trust eliminates the necessity for probate since the person does not own the assets; therefore, there are no probatable assets. A trust costs money and takes time to create, but probate also takes time and costs money. In some cases, the cost may be similar. It's the timing that is different.

2. At the death of one of the original creators of the trust, the estate immediately transfers (according to the trust's directions) to the next trustee or designated heirs, either the surviving spouse or the next trustee. This means you, as the next trustee (for example), can now manage the assets without waiting for probate to go through its process. The assets are available immediately for any and all the bills. Assets (like the house) can be sold.

Also at this time, any capital assets (real estate, special collections) need an appraisal. If the asset has a capital gain impact, the reassessment at the death of the first trustee adjusts what the capital gain impact will be upon the death of the second grantor. (All this is irrelevant if there is only one grantor or trustee).

You cannot imagine how difficult it is after a parent dies. Going through all his or her things, handling any internal squabbling, deciding on this or that, and then going to court to hash it all out—why do it then, when you are least able to make that level of decision? You are making decisions under duress. Make decisions now. A trust costs at least three thousand. Probate costs a minimum 1 percent of the value of the estate, and it takes at least six months. Why handle issues when you are stressed, sad, and grieving? Handle them when you are able to make good, solid decisions.

Not everyone needs or should have a trust. But you need to talk to an estate-planning lawyer to figure this out. This may be a good time to attend one of those free seminars on estate planning. It may help you decide whether to take it to the next step and set up an appointment with a lawyer. If you own property in more than one state, you should have a trust. If your property is in multiple states and you do not have a trust, your probate process will occur in all the states involved.

We have a trust. We did it because we do not have children. We do have nephews, and we live in a different state than they do. We do not want them to have to figure out all of our finances, go through probate in a different state, and try to figure what we have. So we created a trust. All of our assets are in the trust, and they are named. We have a document that our lawyer created that describes the process after one of us dies and after the second of us dies. We don't care about the public part of it. We just want it easier for our designated secondary trustees to have an easier time of it.

A living revocable trust can be changed during the lifetime of the original creators of the trust. We have changed our trust because of changing circumstances and situations. That's what "revocable" means. You (the original creators of the trust) can change it. Once the originators have died, the trust is no longer able to change, and upon disposition of the assets, it ceases to exist (in most cases). A living revocable trust should contain a complete inventory of assets, clear disposition of assets, an allowance for gifting, a clear process outlined when either one or both creators of the trust die, and an affidavit of trust, which is the document that outlines the critical information that financial institutions will need to retitle your accounts. Directions about how the trust should be maintained are very helpful as you work with the trust. Having a trust makes us feel confident about how things will be handled upon one or both of our deaths. It gives us secure knowledge that we will ease the burden on our agent. Everything is outlined and documented. We did it all while we are able to make decisions thoughtfully and carefully. Since it is revocable, as we go through life, we can change it when appropriate. That makes us feel confident and protected.

Documenting items in your estate certainly does not require a trust. Parents who have documented everything are a blessing to caregivers. You just need to know where the documentation is and if it is up-to-date.

Another way to transfer money is called a payable-upon-death or transfer-up-on-death account. You can set up brokerage and bank accounts to be payable upon death. That eliminates some fears that people have regarding relinquishing control of their assets. The accounts automatically transfer to the person named. For couples, this may work for the first one to die. When the second parent dies, if there are multiple children, this may not work out as well. Check with your bank or an estate-planning lawyer to see if this option will work for your situation.

You should consult an attorney to help you decide what the best course is for you. It's worth the money. But make sure it's a good estate-planning lawyer. Find someone you are comfortable with who advises you the best way for you and your family.

Summary

There are many things to consider with the financial and legal requirements. The simpler the estate, the simpler things become. But as part of the caregiving team for your parents, you need to know the numbers and need to have some idea of what's ahead of you. You cannot plan if you do not know the numbers. You will have much more difficulty handling their finances if the proper paperwork is not done. The earlier you get started, the better job you will be doing for your parents. It's wonderful when the parents have things all planned out. It helps you tremendously, but you need to know what they have planned out and what the stuff is.

If they haven't done any planning, then you need to move things along. You can start with the simple will and the powers of attorney. They may not cost any money. You can start to inventory the assets since some of them may have to be sold to fund your parents' care. Wherever there is a good spot to begin, begin there.

Create your to-do list. Make sure you know where wills, powers of attorney, and possibly trust documents are. If you are an agent, then you need a copy of those documents. If those documents don't exist, get them created. Check your state's official website for "Advanced Directives" and download them. Check your state bar association's website for information on advanced directives, the probate process for your state, and the names of elder law attorneys or estate-planning attorneys. Attend free seminars about estate planning. It will help you.

It's the Eyes

The eyes always got to me. The eyes became lifeless. But it happened slowly. Each time I would visit, more life was gone.

When I'd look into my mother's brown eyes, I would see nothing—no light, no interest, no understanding. It's the eyes. If you want to understand what dementia does to people, look into their eyes. But there's no "into." You just look at their eyes. Their eyes return nothing.

When you look into the eyes of a child, you'll see wonder, excitement, curiosity, love, anger, and every other emotion. Now look into the eyes of a person with dementia. In the early stages, you see lots of confusion, concern, and fear. You see that person trying to understand and make sense out of the world he or she is in. In the later stages, you see blankness.

The eyes—empty, blank, lifeless. You see this loss every time you see the person. Even when you bring chocolates, and he or she likes chocolates; he or she smiles and indulges him- or herself—and then you look at the eyes. Nothing. There is a smile on the face but no smile in the eyes.

Where's that curiosity that used to be there? Where's the competiveness? Where's the world-awareness? Where's the next book to read? Where's the newspaper spread out? Where's the crossword puzzle partially done with the dictionary next to the paper?

Gone.

Where's the fierce pride and the poor self-image? Where's the athlete? Where are the golf clubs? Where's that blazing walking speed? And red, where's the red, the favorite color?

Where's the knife that cut all the fat off of meat? Where's the dried-out beef roast because one must cook everything until every last bit of moisture is gone? Where's the "I hate cooking"? Where's the infamous casserole? Where is all of that? Gone.

And it's not in the eyes.

CHAPTER 6
Dementia

Definition

According to *Miriam-Webster's Online Dictionary*, Dementia is a: "…usually progressive condition (as Alzheimer's disease) marked by deteriorated cognitive functioning often with emotional apathy," and Dictionary.com defines it as, "severe impairment or loss of intellectual capacity and personality integration, due to the loss of or damage to neurons in the brain."

There are many causes of dementia, Alzheimer's being the leading one.

Causes of Dementia

- Alzheimer's
- Lewy body
- Parkinson's
- alcohol
- stress
- strokes
- and many more

Alzheimer's and dementia are not the same. However, those two words are often used interchangeably. *Alzheimer's* is the word of the day and is often the easy route to declare what's wrong. Currently, the only true way to tell that it's Alzheimer's disease is to do a brain autopsy. Diagnostic techniques are improving, and I believe there will soon be a definitive way to state that Alzheimer's is the cause of the dementia without the person having to die to prove it.

Alzheimer's is the leading cause of dementia, so the attention to it is appropriate. And right now, it is incurable—meaning that the dementia is progressive, it doesn't stop, and there is no way to cure it. Alzheimer's is fatal. Some medications slow it down, and some approaches currently look like they will slow it down, but nothing stops it yet.

So if it doesn't stop, then you need to plan and prepare for what is going to happen.

It's terrible to watch. Usually you, as a family member, don't even know what is happening. You are confused and can't explain the activities or behaviors of your parent—misplacing and losing things, the inability to make a decision, and the inability to figure out what to do next. There is no initiative, no ability anymore to solve a problem. And it frustrates you, the caregiver.

Reality check: If your parents can't find things and can't figure out things, how are they going to manage their medications, manage their finances, or manage their health needs? They can't. If there is a spouse, that spouse may be covering for the advancement of the dementia or be so overwhelmed he or she doesn't know what to do (stress). It's so difficult to watch the loss of your loved one's life as dementia takes over. Most likely, without other medical issues, this individual will end up in a nursing home (or memory care facility). Plan for it.

In the advanced stages, the individual should go into a nursing home. The mild stages are the most difficult because there are very lucid days, and the person seems fine some of the time. But the day-to-day work of living becomes more and more difficult for him or her. The individual knows that something is not right and will cover it up. The methods and means of the cover-up are artful and clever.

Here are some indications of what the stages contain. Taken from the Alzheimer's Association website (www.alz.org), this is the current thinking on the stages and the definitions of those stages of Alzheimer's. These stages and definitions may become further refined over time.

Caution: People progress through Alzheimer's differently. Stages may overlap with symptoms coming from contiguous stages, or the symptoms may not occur at all. My mother never wandered, as an example of a symptom that didn't occur. You've probably blown past stages 1 and 2. It's just not obvious. Then, more direct indications are noticeable, starting at the mild stages, 3 and 4. In stage 5, you, the caregiver, will get very nervous and have difficulty understanding what's happening to the person with dementia, unless the person has been diagnosed with dementia. For stages 6 and 7, the person should be in a nursing home. You cannot take care of him anymore. It's too difficult. If you are in a position to continue to help him, it means that you have moved in with him or he has moved in with you. You have quit your job, and take care of that person 24/7. Most people are not able to do that.

Taken from the Alzheimer's Association website, alz.org, the stages and definitions of those stages are:

Stage 1: No impairment
Stage 2: Very mild decline
Stage 3: Mild decline
Stage 4: Moderate decline
Stage 5: Moderately severe decline
Stage 6: Severe decline
Stage 7: Very severe decline

Stage 1: No impairment (normal function)

The person does not experience any memory problems. An interview with a medical professional does not show any evidence of symptoms of dementia.

Stage 2: Very mild cognitive decline (may be normal age-related changes or earliest signs of Alzheimer's disease)

The person may feel as if he or she is having memory lapses—forgetting familiar words or the location of everyday objects. But no symptoms of dementia can be detected during a medical examination or by friends, family, or coworkers.

Stage 3: Mild cognitive decline (early-stage Alzheimer's can be diagnosed in some, but not all, individuals with these symptoms)

Friends, family, or coworkers begin to notice difficulties. During a detailed medical interview, doctors may be able to detect problems in memory or concentration. Common stage 3 difficulties include

- noticeable problems coming up with the right word or name;
- trouble remembering names when introduced to new people;
- having noticeably greater difficulty performing tasks in social or work settings, and forgetting material that one has just read;
- losing or misplacing a valuable object; and
- increasing trouble with planning or organizing.

Stage 4: Moderate cognitive decline (Mild or early-stage Alzheimer's disease)

At this point, a careful medical interview should be able to detect clear-cut symptoms in several areas:

- forgetfulness of recent events
- impaired ability to perform challenging mental arithmetic—for example, counting backward from 100 by 7s
- greater difficulty performing complex tasks, such as planning dinner for guests, paying bills, or managing finances
- forgetfulness about one's own personal history
- becoming moody or withdrawn, especially in socially or mentally challenging situations

Stage 5: Moderately severe cognitive decline (Moderate or midstage Alzheimer's disease)

Gaps in memory and thinking are noticeable, and individuals begin to need help with day-to-day activities. At this stage, those with Alzheimer's may

- be unable to recall their own address or telephone number or the high school or college from which they graduated;
- become confused about where they are or what day it is;
- have trouble with less challenging mental arithmetic, such as counting backward from 40 by subtracting 4s or from 20 by 2s;
- need help choosing proper clothing for the season or the occasion;
- still remember significant details about themselves and their family; and
- still require no assistance with eating or using the toilet.

Stage 6: Severe cognitive decline (Moderately severe or midstage Alzheimer's disease)

Memory continues to worsen, personality changes may take place, and individuals need extensive help with daily activities. At this stage, individuals may

- lose awareness of recent experiences as well as of their surroundings;
- remember their own name but have difficulty with their personal history;
- distinguish familiar and unfamiliar faces but have trouble remembering the name of a spouse or caregiver ;
- need help dressing properly and may, without supervision, make mistakes, such as putting pajamas over daytime clothes or shoes on the wrong feet;
- experience major changes in sleep patterns—sleeping during the day and becoming restless at night;
- need help handling details of toileting (for example, flushing the toilet, wiping, or disposing of tissue properly);
- have increasingly frequent trouble controlling their bladder or bowels;
- experience major personality and behavioral changes, including suspiciousness and delusions (such as believing that their caregiver is an impostor) or compulsive, repetitive behavior like hand-wringing or tissue shredding; and tend to wander or become lost.

Stage 7: Very severe cognitive decline (Severe or late-stage Alzheimer's disease)

In the final stage of this disease, individuals lose the ability to respond to their environment, to carry on a conversation, and, eventually, to control movement. They may still say words or phrases.

At this stage, individuals need help with much of their daily personal care, including eating or using the toilet. They may also lose the ability to smile, to sit without support, and to hold their heads up. Reflexes become abnormal. Muscles grow rigid. Swallowing is impaired. They could choke to death.

So what do these stages mean to you? It's a way of recognizing where along the continuum your parent is. It's a way to describe to doctors or caregivers what the possible specifics of your parent's condition are. However, you will not remember whether a symptom is in stage 3 or 5. Alzheimer's can be thought of as mild, moderate, and advanced. The mild stages are difficult for individuals who have the disease. They will recognize that something isn't right. The moderate stages become more problematic as the daily living tasks do not get done and more caregiving and organizing by you is required. In the advanced stages, safety must be a concern and admitting them to a memory care center or nursing home becomes a reality.

The first thing that you can do is help get your parent evaluated. There are some simple tests that prove that dementia exists. Gerontologists (doctors for the over seventy-five crowd) are well aware of these tests, and the tests do not take long. If you really have to figure out if it's Alzheimer's, there are locations in the country that do very extensive testing. Sometimes the individual can join a study, and the tests, evaluations, and treatments might be free or at a reduced cost. But the diagnosis of dementia can be incorporated into the annual or semiannual medical exam or just a special doctor's visit. If you are able, call the doctor's office ahead of time and ask that your parent be tested for dementia.

If the onset of dementia happens fast, then it isn't Alzheimer's. It may be the result of small strokes, it may be a urinary tract infection, or it may even be a reaction the individual is having to medications. That is why your parent needs to be evaluated. It might not be a lasting dementia. It may be the result of some other cause. Strokes do cause dementia, but if there is never another stroke, then the level of dementia does not increase (unless there are other underlying causes). With a stroke and quick attention to it, the individual may regain most or all of the memories.

In reality, if lasting dementia is present, what difference does it make what caused it? You have to deal with the dementia regardless of the cause. Most doctors prescribe similar medications for the individual regardless of the cause of the dementia. Aricept and Namenda are two used frequently. During the final stage of the dementia, talk with the doctor to get your parent off the drugs. It's too late for the drugs to have any further positive effect. These drugs do not cure Alzheimer's or any other dementia. They may help reduce symptoms.

But here are things that you can do to help people with dementia. These steps can be started in the mild stages, stage 3 and 4. Definitely should be used by stage 5 and beyond.

- Simplify the environment of the person with dementia. Remove clutter from living space, cupboards, and closets. Help clean out different areas so that the important, everyday items are easily spotted and reachable.

- Shorten your sentences. People with dementia understand maybe 25 percent of what you say by the time they reach stage 3 or 4. That means for every four words you speak, they understand one word. Use short words. Use short sentences. Use short explanations. They can no longer follow a long and rambling explanation.

- As you talk to them, show pictures of what you mean or point to the item. Don't make them struggle with guessing what you mean. This isn't a contest. It's trying to ease their confusion and help them relax.

- Label drawers, shelves, closets, and bathrooms so they don't need to struggle to figure out what is in which drawer or cupboard. Initially they can still read.

- Don't argue with them. You cannot win any arguments with them, and it makes them nervous, edgy, and uncomfortable. They do not understand what you are trying to say anyway, or they are interpreting what you are saying differently. They just don't get what you are saying.

- Redirect conversations, activities, and motion. This is where dementia helps you. Their attention span is short. Redirecting often calms them or gets them moving in the direction you need them to go. Just switch topics in conversation, turn the page in a magazine, and point to something different. Change the current focus. Sometimes the person with dementia (PWD) will become obsessed with something or some event, and it becomes harder to redirect at this point. But keep trying. Something is triggering the reaction, and you just have to go with it. The person will sense your frustration. PWDs sense emotion. They are struggling to make sense of their very confused world. If they strike out in some way, something is wrong in their world. You need to figure it out, if you can.

- Ensure their safety. Most likely, you will decide to move them to a facility when their safety or that of others becomes an issue. Hide the car keys, unplug the stove, and turn down the water heater. Make sure you have a key to the house. Arrange furniture, knickknacks, and rugs so that they do not hinder the individual. Keep things simple, uncluttered, and quiet.

- Take away or hide the checkbook, credit card, and debit card. They can no longer handle their finances. They will not be able to distinguish between a debit and credit card.

- Watch their phone bills. My mother could not distinguish between the TV remote controller and the phone. There were many strange phone calls to equally strange locations. Label each item.

- Don't let them drive. They will get lost, and they will get scared. It isn't right to put someone else in danger because you are trying to preserve your loved one's ego or feelings. The person with dementia will get over it. He or she will forget. We hid the keys from my mother. We all knew where the car keys were. My mother, who had dementia, seemed to feel more secure when she could see the car. That helped her. But we couldn't let her drive. One of the things that my parents figured out during my mother's early stage of dementia was that she could still drive but couldn't find places. My father couldn't drive anymore but did remember where things were and how to get there. So my mother would get my father into the car, and he would direct her where to turn, where to stop (and how to stop), and when to go. Thank God they lived in a small town. Comforting, isn't it?

- Don't ever ask them, "Do you remember?" How cruel this question is.

- Develop and hone your patience.

- Reduce the options to two simple ones as in "Red or blue?" or "Coffee or tea?"

- Always introduce yourself. "Hi, Mom, it's Janine." Remember that this isn't about you; it's about the person with dementia.

- Approach them slowly and with a smile. They react positively to smiles.

PWDs lose some of their cultural recognition layers. They forget that there are certain cultural taboos around what you normally wouldn't do or say. Sometimes what comes out of their mouths is very funny and very politically incorrect. Again, they can sense emotions. They can sense your censorship or disgust. They may not understand where the emotions are coming from, but they know if there is anger and frustration and will respond negatively to those. PWDs are always responding to something. It's our job to try to figure out what it is. Most of the time, we are not successful. Think about what you do or say if something is distressing you. What is distressing you could be physical, emotional, or mental. You act out because of it. You may just complain to a good friend, curse under your breath, or take a long walk. Well, PWDs have the same issues. Their channeling of their issue just doesn't make sense to us. It gets mistranslated going from the emotion to the brain.

Try to recognize within yourself that you also are having problems with dementia, not yours, but with your parents'. This early and midstage Alzheimer's takes a toll on the caregiver. At first, the lack of understanding, the lack of knowledge, and the confusion that you, the caregiver, have are difficult and frustrating. Your inability to fix this problem becomes apparent, and you may feel helpless and alone. You also need help.

PWDs are also very trusting, especially if the person has a smile or is friendly and helpful. My mother couldn't find her way home from where she voted one November day. The place where my folks voted was two blocks from their house and within view of their house. After walking to the voting place, voting, and then turning around to go back home, my mother got confused. She didn't know where she was or how to get home. However, thank God, one of my former high school classmates saw my mother's confusion and growing fear. This classmate recognized my mother and offered to drive her back home. My mother didn't have a clue who this person was. She just got in the car, and my classmate drove my mother back home. Thank you, former classmate, but that was a bit scary—probably for my classmate too. But my mother was so trusting. My classmate told me of the incident when we ran into each other at the grocery store. Thank you for telling me. It is important to know.

Your local Alzheimer's Association has support, help, and courses in how to handle this. If you have time, you should take advantage of all the help and support you can get your hands on. They understand what you are going through and can help you with your issues, present and future. A nursing home in your area may hold seminars or classes. If you can, take them. It will help. You will find a network of people all going through the same thing. Compare notes, cry together, and laugh together.

Locate a memory care facility, and go through it. Find out what activities they do. Do not settle for a facility that just babysits everyone. That's the wrong perspective. People with dementia are still functioning adults. They still want to contribute. They still have energy. Let them participate in each day—even if it means folding towels (again and again) or frosting cookies.

Once your loved one is in a care facility, decide under what conditions you would have him or her admitted to a hospital. The hospital is especially difficult for a person with dementia. If your parent has an advanced stage of dementia, I recommend them never going to a hospital. You may not be able to help it though. Hospitals are not equipped to deal with advanced dementia patients. PWDs cannot express themselves; they cannot tell you what's wrong or what hurts. They are surrounded by too many people, too much hustle, and too much noise in a hospital. It is extraordinarily disturbing to them. Both my mother and mother-in-law were admitted to hospitals for very good reasons, and the results were disastrous. My mother had suffered a heart attack. She never felt anything, just collapsed one day at the nursing home. She had her own room at the hospital. They got her plugged into all the equipment and got her stabilized (medically speaking). After the staff left the room, she tore out all the plugs, IVs, or whatever else she was attached to; got up out of the bed; and ran out of the room. My mother could really move fast. She was frightened out of her mind. She had no comprehension of what was happening. The nurses ran after her and put her back into the room. Then they barricaded the door slightly. And what was the outcome? The result of the hospital visit and tests conducted on her was that we weren't going to put her through surgery to unblock the artery. We weren't going to do anything to an almost ninety-year-old woman with advanced dementia. What was the purpose? To see what was wrong? It was a horrible experience for her and the hospital staff. After that, we directed the nursing home not to ever take her to the hospital again. We couldn't think of any good reason to admit her. And the hospital was only doing their job.

PWDs have vestiges of their lives buried within them. They react when that vestige is in front of them. My mother's favorite color was always red. When she broke her arm and needed a cast, the doctor asked me what color she should have, and I said, "Red." She then responded with, "Red is my favorite color." By the way, she didn't even know she had broken her arm. She waved it around and said, "It's not broken." But she left with a red cast.

Dementia means the loss of functionality. Functionality is that ability to do things properly. One area of functionality that my mother lost early on was the ability to distinguish between hot and cold. She would stand out in the middle of the road in winter and look for the garbage trucks to come—no coat, hat, boots, or any protection. Either a neighbor or a passerby would walk her inside, frozen. She did not know that she was cold. The brain pathway was broken. Her body never got the news that she was cold.

She would put on water for tea and not be able to tell whether the water or the burner was hot. This functionality was the reason we eventually removed my parents from their home. She started a fire in the house. She had no concept of what was dangerous (e.g., electricity).

A person with dementia has difficulty taking a shower. When you take your next shower, mentally catalog all the decisions, reactions, and movements you use when showering. PWDs cannot process all of that stimuli as quickly as they need to in order to take a shower. The noise, the water on the body, the water in the eyes, and reaching for the soap or the washcloth become impossible for them to manage. I read an article written by a woman with earlier-onset Alzheimer's about taking a shower. It was an extraordinary description of what it feels like and how difficult this simple task (or we think that it's simple) is. They need help.

PWDs lose their ability to know the time. They cannot judge how long something takes to do. They forget what month, day, or year it is. Sometimes they lose the ability to tell whether they are hungry or not. My mother-in-law had that issue. She started to eat constantly. It is so much easier to put them on a strict schedule. It becomes consistent and predictable. Decisions don't have to be made. It makes them feel safe. It makes them feel protected.

Many PWDs have sundowner's syndrome. My mother had that. When the sun goes down, they get edgy and nervous. There isn't much to do about that except keep them busy during that time and get them to bed. Did you know that PWDs are more tired than the rest of us? They are struggling all day to understand their environment, to make sense of this chaotic world they are in, and they wear themselves out. So they sleep more. Observe their sleep patterns.

And then, of course, there is the full-moon effect. The full-moon effect creates a nervousness or restlessness for a PWD. My sister would purposely go to the Alzheimer's ward at my mother's nursing home the late afternoon of a full moon and help the staff out. She would help with the evening meal and then try to keep the residents occupied or distracted while the staff helped get everyone settled and in bed. Sometimes it worked.

Some dementia sufferers get obsessive about different things. This comes in the earlier stages. They may want to do the same thing over and over again or say the same thing over and over. One woman kept repeating this story about a neighbor who was a child abuser. This was a memory from her childhood. She kept repeating the story, and it wasn't pleasant. You could stop her for a while. After that, she would just start over again. This story obviously had embedded itself in her brain at an early age.

Reactions to everyday life become stilted or even nonexistent. PWDs are trying to process what's occurring but can't quite make the normal connection any more. It's not that they don't feel anything; they don't know what they are feeling. You should expect some strange reactions or at least unanticipated ones. If someone has told them something, they simply may not have understood the words used or not understand the implications of those words.

As an example, when my mother-in-law's doctor was diagnosing her dementia, one of the items they did was take a blood test to see if there was anything organically wrong with her. The doctor had immediately put her on Aricept. She received the results of the blood test in the mail. Doctors are looking for an abnormal blood work in case the dementia symptoms are a result of something chemically wrong. Then if medications are screwing up the individual, the medications can be altered or eliminated and the symptoms of dementia relieved. However, in my mother-in-law's case, scrawled across her blood test results were, "Blood tests all normal." My in-laws were thrilled. "All normal." Well, my mother-in-law had also written on the back of that results page, "Thank goodness for Aricept." She decided that she was normal and nothing was wrong. No dementia. My father-in-law wanted to believe it too. This is one case where you want something to be wrong with the blood work.

Mild Cognitive Impairment

Researchers and the medical community have recently, within the past few years, identified a stage called mild cognitive impairment (MCI). It is identified as a stage possibly pre-Alzheimer's. The "possibly" is because there aren't enough studies on mild cognitive impairment yet. Some individuals seem to stay in the MCI stage for some time while others advance to Alzheimer's rather quickly. As with Alzheimer's, there is no known reason why this occurs. MCI results in memory issues that are minor but more significant than "I can't find my keys." A person with MCI can be diagnosed by his or her doctor with some memory issues and put on the standard Alzheimer's medication. This seems to be more effective in slowing memory loss. Preliminary results indicate this. People with MCI are quite high-functioning. They can drive, and they can hold a job. It's just that sometimes things don't seem right with them. Besides their cognitive lapses, they may also be more obsessive about a topic or subject or something incorporated into their daily living. It may be some activity, like checking the tire pressures for their car every few hours. Another possible physical change is their gait. In one study, about 25 percent of people with MCI changed how they walked. It's easy to understand. The connection between the individual's perceptions of space becomes more difficult to process. There are so many assessments we make so quickly that we don't think about it. When crossing a street or walking down the sidewalk, you make decisions quickly and readily. Stepping off of a curb is second nature to you but may not be to people with dementia or with MCI. They may not be able to perceive the change in height or color that should trigger a reaction to modify their step.

Another change is their perception of time. Things that happened one year ago, in their minds, may be two years ago or six months ago. They are not able to figure out time frames. How long will this take? They cannot figure out everything that needs to be done to prepare for an extended activity. So they begin simplifying their lives. They don't go out as much, they don't do as much, and they don't stimulate their minds as much. They atrophy. They have too much stimulation anyway, so they rely on things and situations that make them feel safe and secure.

As usual, the earlier they are diagnosed and treated the better. In one study, early treatment and early diagnosis resulted in five years of additional functionality. With the possibility of advanced dementia, adding five years of functionality to a person's life is a blessing. Do not mistake adding five years of functionality with adding five years of life to the individual. It's not the same. Keeping functionality makes it easier for both the people with dementia and the people surrounding them.

If you suspect mild cognitive impairment, don't avoid it. You could really help someone early. And maybe within that five years of added functionality, there might be better medication that truly slows down this process of losing one's functioning mind. Wouldn't you want that for yourself?

I have found the local Alzheimer's and dementia organizations to be enormously helpful in explaining the diseases and supporting families going through this. The classes that explain how to prepare, how to recognize symptoms, and how to help are invaluable. Their helplines can support you and get you through this. I volunteered for my local Alzheimer's organization and went to different health fairs. Some people would always find the information and some direction for their next steps. Others would quickly pass by the booth, not wanting to even bring the word *Alzheimer's* anywhere close to them. I understand that.

I found a book, *Aging with Grace* by Dr. David Snowdon, that does a beautiful job of discussing aging and also dementia. The author studied Notre Dame nuns in the United States and followed them for years, documenting how they dealt with aging. Since the environmental factors of the lives of these nuns were similar (diet, work ethic, religious affiliation, and so on), he was able to more closely study the effects of aging on a population and came up with some very interesting results. It's a lovely book. It is one of the earliest books on a study of Alzheimer's as a remarkable expanded study of aging. I highly recommend this book. There are websites relating to some of the results or observations regarding this study of nuns. Dr. Snowdon was also able to look at the early lives of these nuns and formed some telling observations of how early life affects one's ability to age and its possible affect upon getting Alzheimer's.

Summary

- Get your parent evaluated. Call the doctor ahead of time and ask for a test for dementia.
- Simplify your parents' life.
- Take over their bill-paying and other organizational items at their home.
- Don't argue with them.
- Speak in simple sentences and simple words.
- They react to their environment, and it's up to you to figure out what is bothering them.
- Always introduce yourself to them on the phone and in person.
- Approach with a smile. Develop patience.
- Create a safe environment for them.
- Find a nursing home, memory care facility, or care facility that handles dementia.
- Get support from your local Alzheimer's or dementia organization.

CHAPTER 7
How to Keep Focused

How do you stay focused when everything is collapsing in front of you? How do you stay focused as all your competing priorities bear down on you?

It's very difficult, but these are some principles to keep in mind as you proceed along your caregiving journey. These principles helped me to stay focused.

Principles

1. Make decisions based on what's best for your parents.
2. Maintain family relationships.
3. Communicate with all family members.

Having these principles helps you focus on the most important items and gets rid of all the extraneous issues impacting your emotions and your efforts. It helps to keep you going and helps you know what you need to do. Let's look at each of these principles and see what they mean in practical terms.

Make decisions based on what's best for your parents. Focus on them.

Always ask yourself this question: "What decision can I make that is best for my parents right now?" This question maintains proper focus; it's about the parents. What is going to help them the most right now? This doesn't mean that you drop all your other priorities, like your own family (spouse, children) or your job. It is a horrible balancing act. So when you ask yourself the question, "What's best for the parents?" the next question or issue is, "How does it get done?" It is the decision of what needs to be done and how it gets done that drives every next step. Who it gets done by is the third question.

What limits do you have? Do you know to what length you can go to support your parents? You may not know what that limit is yet, but you will find out. When you have competing priorities, you need to understand, from your perspective, what is most important to you. And if your parents are not your first priority (your spouse or children may take that spot), then you must be prepared to make some choices that will not have you helping your parents in particular situations. I knew right away that I could not have my parents (or my in-laws) live with us. I knew that I couldn't take that. Is that considered selfish? By some, I'm sure. However, how selfish is it if you know that you are going to be miserable, your spouse is going to be miserable, and your parents are going to know that and sense that? In that case, is this the best decision for your parents? No. Some think that it is your obligation to have your parents move in with you or you with them. In some cases, and yours may be one of them, that does make sense. You have the right relationship, and you have the right space. It can work for you. You may be very lucky if that is the case. A friend of mine had her mother live with her during the last year of her mother's life. They had a marvelous relationship, and my friend was single. The mother and daughter enjoyed that time together, and her mother died peacefully at the end of that year. My friend was so grateful for that time and was so lucky to be able to offer that option for her elderly mother. My friend was very blessed and very lucky.

For other family dynamics, that doesn't make sense. One person that I knew did have her mother-in-law move in with them temporarily. It seemed to make sense, and she felt that it was an obligation and that it was the right thing to do. It became horrible for her and her husband. As kind and good as these people were, having the mother-in-law there was so disruptive and stressful that she made the decision not to offer the same option to her parents. She didn't realize before this experience how much stress this added to her and her husband's life.

At one point during very serious issues with his parents, my husband said, "What else can I do?" He was doing everything that he could. There really wasn't anything else he could do except for him to move in with his parents. That would mean he would have to either take an extended leave from work or quit. So I proposed it to him. If he felt that strongly about helping his folks at the next level, then that was what he should do. He decided against that. There is a limit to what you can do. You may not know initially what that limit is, but you will find it out. Whatever that limit is, it is okay. If you are honestly supporting your parents to the best of your ability within the constraints of your life, then your limit is okay.

A question that sometimes is helpful is: "Am I doing this for any reason other than helping my folks?" Are you doing this so you can look good to your siblings or your coworkers? Or because you like being a martyr? This isn't about what other people think or believe; this is about what you believe. This is about what would be helpful for your parents. If you are doing it for other reasons than helping your parents, then there is additional stress on you and your life because the motivation is not honest.

But remember: you cannot do everything. You cannot fix a lifelong set of decisions that were made by your parents that contributed to their current situation.

For example, I worked with an elderly woman as her representative payee, the person who manages someone else's Social Security money. In this case, that was all the income and money that she had. And the reason that was all the money and income she had was because of her previous seventy-plus years of bad decision making. I couldn't help that situation; I had to deal with what was existing at the time. It's too bad, but there wasn't going to be any other money, so we had to deal with it. It happens. It was her current reality.

You cannot change their personalities or their conditions. You can only support them to the best of your ability to make them safe or make them more comfortable. If they refuse, then that's all you can do. Just be there for them when they need help—and tell them that. Say to them, "If you need some help, you let me know." After some very contentious arguments with my husband's parents, we came up with that approach. If they keep refusing, then instead of arguing with them, acknowledge that refusal with an offer to help when they ask. Yes, you have to hold your breath and wait for the phone call that is the next disaster, but it is still their life. It is still their decision. It is still them wanting to control their own life even if their decisions are bad. You cannot fix everything. You cannot make all of this go away. And yes, you have to live with the fear, the helplessness, and the anxiety of not being there and not doing anything some of the time.

When talking to siblings or other interested parties, always come back to "What's best for the parents right now?" If possible, include your parents in the conversation—if it makes sense. But you also need to let your parents know what you are thinking and what you are concerned about. They may be able to help. Or they may completely ignore you or chastise you. When talking to your siblings, ask them for their opinions regarding your folks. Include them, if it makes sense. Don't predict what they are going to say or what their reaction will be. Regardless, come back to what makes sense right now and what can be done right now that is the best for your parents.

Maintain family relationships.

Synonyms of *maintain* include *uphold*, *preserve*, *keep*, *continue*, *sustain*, and *conserve*.

If you are the major caregiver, then one of your responsibilities is to maintain family relationships. This does assume there is a family relationship in existence. It doesn't mean that you are responsible for improving or creating all family relationships or making them wonderful. When a parent has aged and needs support, then it's the family that should be rallying. Not all family members can rally. Not all family members are able to help. Not all family members want to help. Whatever your situation is, just don't make it worse. Maintain.

If the focus is your parents, then other siblings deserve to know what's happening. If you are the most knowledgeable about the situation, remember that the rest of the family is not. The rest of the family isn't in the same physical, mental, or psychological spot that you are. Their initial reaction to news or to a crisis is going to be different than yours. If you are involved and they are not, how can you expect the same level of knowledge or acceptance? Give them time and give them information. Give them some slack. But keep them informed. If they criticize you, just ignore it or take a deep breath. You need to keep them informed. You need to make sure they have the information that you have. They can make their own decisions about how much they can help. Sometimes you may have to assign them jobs. If they aren't the primary caregiver, as you are, they don't know every detail, schedule, or medication. They don't have the same knowledge or perspective that you have. Most siblings and family members want to help but don't know what to do or what needs to be done. Most of them are also concerned, scared, or overwhelmed. They may strike out at you because you are the messenger. They may try to curry favor with your folks, pit one against the other, or come to their own conclusions about what's right or wrong. And you may receive the brunt of the criticism. You may end up being the bad guy. There usually isn't a bunch of good news here so your messages and other communications aren't cheerful.

Don't get drawn into territorial battles, verbal battles, or bashing of other family members. Let all parties know what is happening and what you are doing or planning to do. Don't leave anyone out.

Some families grow stronger and closer together as a result of the mutual responsibilities of caring for the elderly parents. Some families do not have that result. One of the results of this caregiving for your elderly parents is the strain it imposes upon the family relationships. You will learn something about yourself and your family members. Sometimes what you learn isn't pleasant. Sometimes what happens to the family relationship shows the inherent weaknesses or strengths that are truly part of the family dynamic. And sometimes it hurts to find that out. But if your focus is on doing the best for your parents, the reality of your family dynamic is secondary. Don't let that become the focus. Don't let that rule the decisions. Don't walk away because something unpleasant has happened. You can deal with your family dynamic later. Right now, it's about your parents.

And you also can just as easily be pleasantly surprised. You can find strength or knowledge where you least expected. You may find some support where you didn't even know to look. Those are wonderful gifts. Cherish them, and you may find a helpful secondary caregiver.

If you are not the major caregiver, try to support the major caregiver as much as you can. You need to offload the burden wherever and whenever you can. You need to listen to the major caregiver, lend a hand when and if you can, and trust that the major caregiver is doing the best job he or she can and that he or she has the parents' interest foremost in his or her mind and deeds. Ask the major caregiver, "What can I do?" Offer to do something even if it is cleaning the major caregiver's house. Make him or her dinner. But trust. This isn't about your relationship with the major caregiver; it is about your parents. Help them.

At either level of caregiving, someone may holler at you. Try to find the why of the hollering. What is eating away at this person? It hurts. It is hard. If it is more continuous, ask that person to be the major caregiver if he or she does not believe you are doing the right thing. Tell him or her you will support him or her if he or she chooses to be the major caregiver, and if not, find something of substance that he or she can do. Get the person involved and up to speed, and give him or her something to do (e.g., accompanying the parents to doctors' appointments). Let the person experience what is happening, or invite him or her to spend the weekend with the parents to give him or her firsthand experience with the situation. Clue the person in to what is coming down the road. Ask for help.

Just because an involved family member has a certain job or certain knowledge (e.g., a lawyer or a doctor) does not mean that he or she is the best choice for a caregiver. Caregiving is a daily activity with daily chores. Lawyers and doctors are great advisors and great help with certain jobs that need to be done, but they may not be the best choice as the caregiver. Their knowledge may actually get in the way of doing what's best for the parents. The egos of individuals, including yours, may have to be injured in the caregiving job. The egos have to take a backseat now. They cannot be the reason things are done or not done.

At the end of your caregiving duties, reflect upon what you have witnessed. Reflect upon your family and what its strengths are. Acknowledge the weaknesses, but don't let them interfere with your relationships with your family. It's still your family. Maybe the relationships have shifted, but that's okay. Just continue to relate. You might need them.

Communicate with all family members.

If you are the major caregiver, you do have the responsibility to do the communicating. You can decide on the best method: e-mails, voice, texts, instant messaging, or letters. Different methods work for different people. Copies of all pertinent documents (health care power of attorney and financial power of attorney) should be given to family members, even if they are not the specific agents. I have a copy of my sister's health care power of attorney even though I am not named as one of her agents. But I know who is named as her agents. I am an interested party, and I can work with her agents if I should notice anything and they do not. I can work with her agents if they ask me for information or help. I know who they are, and I know that they have my sister's best interests at heart. Don't be afraid of sharing information.

As the major caregiver, you can have someone else do the communications, someone who would like to help but maybe cannot help that much. This person may be well suited to let everyone know the next event or step or what needs to be done. Even if you get criticized or hollered at, keep the communications open and flowing. Someone else may have to step in at some point because you are unable to be there or do whatever needs to be done. If the backup caregiver has been kept informed, it is easier for him or her to step in. If the backups have the data or knowledge, they may be able to help or see where they can help you. Do not fall into the trap of thinking that you are the only one who can do this. There are others.

Sometimes you will slip up. Don't beat yourself up because of it. Stay focused, and keep remembering what the major focus is: *what's best for your parents* (not what's best for your siblings). It isn't easy; in some families, it is impossible to communicate effectively. Try your best. You will learn some things, and you will know that you tried. Know that not communicating is not helping.

Also, you will have conflicting priorities. This was one of mine. As mentioned earlier, my husband and I were the major caregivers for his parents. All the proverbial wheels were off their wagon, and then my mother was dying. It was her last week of life. My sisters and I stayed on vigil at her room at the nursing home for that last week. Two days before she died, my father-in-law fell and broke his ribs. He used a walker and tripped over some clothes on the floor. My mother-in-law was in mid-stage dementia and couldn't help. When I called my husband late on that Thursday evening right before my mother died, he told me about the fall. His father had a doctor's appointment the following Tuesday at 8:30 a.m. to have his ribs looked at. All I said to my husband was, "I can't do anything." I couldn't help my in-laws or my husband. My mother did die the next day, and her funeral was on the following Monday. I abandoned my responsibilities to my husband's family for that week. I expected my husband to miss my mother's funeral because of what was happening to his parents, and that did not bother me in the least. There is just so much that you can do, and being in two places at once is not one of them. My husband did make it to the funeral; he assigned his brother to accompany his father to the doctor's appointment. Conflicting priorities? Couldn't help out? Yes. Hard, yes. At wit's end, yes. But we continued.

Focus, maintain, and communicate. These will help you function during this journey. Also ask your siblings to do the same. Have them communicate with you as well. What are their schedules? What can they do? What do they know? Include them and thank them.

In the end, at the funeral, you want to be standing with your family.

CHAPTER 8
Planning

Planning takes time, effort, and patience. In my work, which is project management, I have found that planning ends up saving time, money, effort, and stress. It works. This elderly parent project is fluid. Things can change in an instant. So how can you plan or organize for something that isn't a static project? And how can you plan for something you know little about? How do you even know where to start or what to plan for? How do you take apart this huge issue into manageable pieces? How do you even get started?

I hope some of the following will help.

In project management, there are formal steps for the life of a project. These are generally considered the steps:

- initiation
- planning or design
- production or execution
- monitoring and controlling
- closing

Sounds intimidating? Overkill? Too formal? Too officious? Let's take these standard project management terms and apply them to the elderly parent issue. Know ahead of time that strict rules do not apply here because of the nature of the issue. It's fluid and changes quickly or sometimes over time. But looking at the structure of a project may help you create a framework for yourself and your family.

Initiation: The Beginning, The Start

You've started. You are initiating. How do I know that? You are reading this book. You are trying to find out what you know and don't know. You are trying to understand the scope of the issues. You are overwhelmed by the enormity of it all and cannot grasp how these issues came to be or how to handle them. You are unclear if you can handle these things but know that there is something you need to do and are responsible for doing. That's the initiation phase. You are analyzing, gathering information, and trying to understand the current situation. You are beginning to grasp the financial implications or at least know that there are financial implications and wondering what kind of help there is for all of this.

That's the initiation phase. You've started your plan.

This planning isn't like a formal project plan. Writing the plan down may help you with communications or setting expectations of siblings or just keeping yourself organized. Writing things down may help you stay focused and moving forward, even though you feel that you are moving backward at times. Writing things down also helps you remember. Making lists helps you focus and can make the feeling of uselessness abate as you cross things off the list or mark the items as done. The feeling of not doing anything or not doing enough permeates the caregiving process. Just know because of these ideas, that you are doing something.

But the written plan isn't necessary. Some items need to be written down, like a will or the names of the doctors or medications. If you work better when you write things down, then write things down. Make a list of items you need to find out (see the medical quiz from chapter 2).

As in the previous chapter on focusing, you need to understand what your goals are, although your goals may change or evolve over time. Think through what you want to accomplish (Survive? Effectively manage your parents' money so they can be taken care of either at home or in a facility? Make it through the next month?). What's the focus here?

This is the initiation phase. As with regular project management, when the scope of the issues changes, you may have to revisit some new issues to scope them out.

Planning or Design Phase

Planning can save you time, stress, and money. It helps set the stage for what's imminent and gives you an ability to respond to whatever happens much more quickly, assuredly, and helpfully. Here's an example of how some prior planning and executing tasks helped us. When the SWAT team arrived at my in-laws' house, we had called the neighbors to inform them of what was occurring; we could do that because we had a list of their names and phone numbers. Prior planning and execution of a task, it helped the neighbors and us.

Your planning here has several aspects. Drawing on all previous chapters will help you get started. You need to identify your team, the set of people who are going to help you. You need to identify who can help with what and when he or she can help. This is that gathering of all the information that each person knows. This is talking to those people to understand where they are in this process and what you can expect of them. Document what is worth documenting. This is identifying what you don't know and figuring out how to get the information needed. This is identifying who is going to do what, when they can do it, how much time they can spend, and maybe what some costs are.

Some of the resources you will need are outside resources, like the medical team, the in-home health workers, or Meals on Wheels. How much those items cost needs to be known to assess the monetary restrictions present in your situation. Until some of those items are needed, at this particular time, you may not know these and it might not be worth the time to find out. If there is time, do some Internet searches of this type of help or go to your local senior resources center to get preliminary information. Check your state, county, or city's official website for support for seniors.

All projects have constraints, and all the constraints are the same: people, time, and money. Early in the book, I mentioned having a sibling meeting. This is your project-planning and design meeting.

Be honest. Set expectations realistically. Don't assign a task to someone who doesn't have the time, even if that person has the capability. Don't take on everything just because it all has to be done. There are limits to everything, including you. This is where the major caregiver role is decided, if it can be. Even though it may change over time, this role needs to be identified. The expectations of the other caregivers need to be discussed, as in "What I can expect from the major caregiver in communicating the situation, and what can the major caregiver expect from me?" This also changes over time, so check in every now and then. Maybe something has occurred in someone's life that precludes him or her being able to spend any additional time in support of the elders.

So this is where you take out the medical quiz given earlier in the book or the checklist and start there. What items do you know, and what do you need to find out? If you want to set time frames, go ahead. That may be helpful to some procrastinators out there. The time frames are more difficult to set here because there isn't an established end date for this type of project. But you do need to keep moving on data and information gathering. So if time frames help, then assign them.

Check with your parents to see what planning they have done. My folks were so proud that they had wills. They thought they had everything covered. Maybe fifty years ago, that was true. It isn't anymore. Your parents may have things well organized. You may be very lucky to have parents who have thought ahead. It makes short work of the planning phase. If your parents are organized and have done some substantial planning, then have the conversations about how you can help or how you can plug in. This conversation will help you understand how far along your parents are in planning.

One of the things that you need to find out is where the documents, keys, numbers, or anything else that's pertinent are. My father sat each of us down and told us about their finances. He told us where his safe was and gave us the combination. He was forthcoming with information. My father-in-law was the opposite. He didn't feel it was any of our business. So in that case, when his back was turned, I looked through his papers. I hunted things down without his knowledge. We needed to know, and that's how we accomplished some of the data gathering. The only thing that he shared with his sons was the location of his life insurance policies. He did that right before he had surgery. We were a little taken off guard so we weren't prepared to press the issue about a few other things. This incident was very early on, and they were doing very well at that time, so we blew that opportunity.

Why plan? Why take the time with so many other things that are so much more fun that need planning or doing? Most people don't plan this part of their life. Some people consider it depressing or morbid. It's neither. Your attitude may be morbid or depressing. Planning can help your parents, you, and other family members. Planning can get you through crises that arise. Planning can have decisions made that merely have to be executed depending on what happens. Planning can save you time, money, and stress. Planning can force you to face up to facts. Planning can help you become organized and focused.

When both my mother and father died, their funerals had been planned and paid for. So at each of their deaths, we just did what the specific tasks were, calling relatives, calling the funeral home, setting the date for the funeral, and so on. We didn't have to pick out caskets (done already), write the obituary (done already), and decide on the clothes that each would wear (done already). Then, at the time of their deaths, we could handle and process their deaths without having to deal with these things. We were prepared. When someone close to you dies, there are so many emotions that decision making becomes more difficult than it would be ordinarily. And what's most important during your grieving is being with the people who care; it isn't having to decide which casket to use.

Planning can help you know what to expect and give you a sense of confidence that you will know the next step and be able to handle it. One benefit that I've seen in all my years as a project manager was that if you knew something of what was coming down the road, you were always better able to handle it. Setting expectations in people precludes some of the anxiety or emotional outbursts that can occur. If you know the expectations, you can put yourself in a much better place when the situation actually arises. Without setting expectations, everything seems a surprise. While some surprises are fun and exciting, the surprises during an elderly parent caregiving aren't fun. Maybe having a glimpse of what may be happening in the future won't make you feel so helpless or out of control. Of course, as examples in the book have shown, you cannot always plan for everything (e.g., the SWAT team showing up at the house). But prior planning did help support that event.

And why don't people plan? Especially in this arena, fear and avoidance are primary reasons. People just don't want to face the decline or mortality of either their parents or themselves. Some people may think that this is useless. It isn't. This planning to help your parents doesn't have to be formal, doesn't have to be written down (although some items are definitely worth writing down), and doesn't require a project management tool. You can start small and know that the plan will evolve. Take the major aspects of this process (refer to the chapters in this book as a guide) and get information, data, paperwork, or lists done as the start. Whenever possible, make decisions ahead of time. Too much emotion clouds your ability to make the best decisions. Give yourself space to handle the emotions by planning these things out.

Monitoring and Controlling

Boy, this sounds big-brother-ish, doesn't it? In a regular business project, the project has to be controlled and monitored. There's a feedback loop that is established so that the project manager can identify issues, problems, setbacks, and critical failures early in the process and mitigate those issues before they become too big and cause the project to fail.

You will be doing some of that here but hardly to the extent that you would in business. You want to check on the caregivers. You want to check on the parents. You want to check on the medical team. You want to check on any outside resource people you use. You want to monitor costs of items, including the parents' checkbook.

Did you get the key to the safety deposit box? Okay. Check. Done. Completed.

Since caregiving is fluid, the variables of effort and time become critical. When the parent has a critical health issue all of a sudden, where are the new resources coming from? Where is the money coming from? Who is monitoring the parents, and what is the expected result? Does something have to be modified in the house, or is the parent going into rehab? How's the major caregiver doing? Do you need to jump in and clean his or her house? Who is taking leave from work? Maybe the major caregiver changes at this time.

So who is communicating with whom? The caregiving parties need to be told when events change or morph into something critical.

This part of elderly caregiving is very fluid and not formal. You may not be controlling much, depending on the situation. But keep the communications flowing. Be a part of the communications solution, not the problem.

Executing

Just do the job. Get the job done. Coordinate people and other resources so that the tasks get done when needed. Set expectations correctly, and communicate all issues and activities. Get help when needed. If you are involved with caregiving, either as the major or secondary caregiver, you must communicate what you are doing. People make decisions based on their understanding of events. Why should someone drive five hours to get someplace just to find out that an appointment was moved, people aren't there, or an event happened to change the situation? You need information.

Take those checklists, and get the answers. Right them down if you cannot remember them. Get the emergency document created and posted on the refrigerator. Do the jobs. Or get someone else to do them.

You will be doing a lot of executing. Checking back with siblings or other supportive people is important to make sure you are doing what is expected or necessary.

Your plan consists of gathering a lot of information, documenting what needs to be documented, and communicating with all interested parties. If you know something of what is coming down the road, you can prepare yourself as best you can for that eventuality. If your parent has dementia, he or she most likely will at some time be moved to a facility. Well then, investigate facilities ahead of time. Pick one. Find out the wait times. Meet with siblings (in person or over the Internet or phone) to check up on what's being done, and report what you've done. Pick out the next things that can be accomplished. Sometimes there is a lull. Take that time to read a book and do the next thing on the list.

Closing

The last phase of project management is called the closing. There is no closing on this effort. It just ends at some point (more about that in the next chapter).

Summary

Planning takes time. It takes effort. It can help you during the crises, and it can save you time, money, and stress. Stress will be ever present. Reading this book will help you plan. It lays out for you what you need to know and consider. Throw out those things that don't pertain to you. Be as formal as you want, but always try your best. Focus on what's most important at the time. Write things down that need to be written down. Communicate. Know that other people have gone down this road and understand what this takes. Find them. Have them help you grasp the enormity of your situation.

CHAPTER 9
The End

The end. Sometimes it comes rather quickly. Other times you can't wait for it to come. That's not callous; that's reality. The end can contain relief, grief, loss, and great sadness. The loss of a parent is significant. Even if you didn't like your parent, it still affects you seriously. Pay attention to the feelings. Facing that loss and accepting that loss may take time. That depends on you. Your life was based on that pillar, your parent, in your life. His or her effect on you may be more significant than you realize. Sometimes the grief takes a while to show up. The grief may be triggered by the smallest of details. You may be sitting in a meeting when someone uses a phrase or talks about a location, and the emotions come flooding in. One day, driving home from work four months after my father's death, I thought of that current October day. It was a beautiful day. And then I burst into tears. It took me a while to figure out what was happening. October was the month that I would buy my dad his annual birdseed. I had done it for years. It was his Christmas present. And now, this October, I wouldn't be doing that, and I missed it. So the grief came through. It's often the simple things.

But back to work. There is a lot to do when someone dies. You may be surprised. There are a lot of phone calls to make. No one quite understands how many phone calls you have to make for all of this journey.

Here's your next task: make a list of who you are going to call when your parent dies. I'll wait.

(Fifteen minutes later)

Let's compare lists:

1. family members
2. close friends of your parents
3. distant family members
4. funeral home
5. church
6. your friends
7. life insurance companies
8. pension plan administrators
9. Social Security
10. phone company and cable company to cancel service
11. anyone who is on an appointment list (doctors)
12. clubs, organizations, card-playing buddies
13. neighbors
14. newspapers or other subscriptions to cancel
15. lawyer, accountant, financial planner
16. any in-home help that was used (cleaning, health aides, chore doers)

Now, write down the phone numbers for all of those people, entities, and organizations. Don't have them? If you don't, you may want to start gathering the numbers and gather e-mail addresses.

For family members, I strongly urge you to call them. You can send e-mails or texts. However, sometimes people aren't reading their e-mails or may think that it's spam or their server is down. For whatever reason, not all e-mails get read. Sending e-mails with further information as to when the funeral or visitation or service is set is fine. If you are sending e-mails to work e-mail addresses, it is possible that the person isn't in the office for a while or on vacation.

You have (I hope) picked out the funeral home already and (I hope) planned and paid for the funeral. If not, then that's number two on your list to do. You'll have to meet with the funeral home to figure out the type and size of the funeral you want (or the person wanted). It'll cost the estate about nine thousand dollars for a regular funeral. Prices do vary. The funeral homes provide many wonderful services. A good funeral home will walk you through the next immediate process. They do the contacting with florists, churches, pastors, newspapers, and Social Security. They get the death certificates. You'll need at least six death certificates. Social Security and all life insurance companies need them for their records. Sometimes a phone or cable company will need them because they may not believe that you are telling the truth. Pension administrators may also require them. Get enough—and that means at least six.

You also will need to write an obituary. The funeral home can help you with that. They have formats for standard obits. Or you could write one ahead of time. That's always helpful. Do you have a picture to send to the newspaper for the obituary? Find one. Do you have the clothes that the parent is going to wear (unless of course it is a cremation)? What are you going to do with the jewelry he or she always wore (wedding rings, engagement rings, watches, earrings, and so on)? Picky little details just seem so burdensome at this time.

I know—too many phone calls and too many decisions. There is a lot of work to do. Thinking of these details ahead of time and making decisions earlier takes the pressure off at the time of the death. Deal with these issues ahead of time, and deal with the death at that time.

Funerals

Some people don't want funerals, and some people cannot afford them. Many people have life insurance or term life insurance to pay for a funeral. That's wonderful if you have that available. Even if the funeral is scaled down and is only in one location, it still costs a lot of money. If the person is being cremated, that even costs about four thousand dollars with no funeral. It's expensive. This is why most people have insurance to pay for these expenses. My experience is that the life insurance companies pay out the claim very quickly.

If the funeral has been prepaid, that eases the pressure quite a bit. You still need to meet with the funeral home and address any additional expenditures and the final details of the funeral planning. These details include when to hold the funeral, where to hold the funeral, and who will officiate. If the person is a veteran, did he or she want representatives of his or her branch of service at the grave site?

Currently many funeral homes ask you to provide photographs so that they can put together a slide show showing different aspects of a person's life. It's such a great idea. For my father-in-law's funeral, we had to scramble (we didn't even know where the pictures were) so his weren't as nice a set as for my mother-in-law. As I was going through their pictures after my father-in-law's death, I set aside pictures I thought would evoke the life of my mother-in-law. So when she died, I grabbed that envelope and went through them again. I had them ready for the funeral home. It was a nice tribute. The funeral home we worked with provided us with multiple copies of the tribute to give to close family members. This was included in the price of the funeral. Many families post pictures on a board that is provided by the funeral home. Either way, try to gather some pictures.

Is the person going to be buried? Is there a cemetery plot? Which cemetery? Even if a person is cremated, some families bury the urn. You need to know and arrange the purchase of a plot if your family doesn't have one. You also need a stone of some sort, depending on your budget, that identifies the individual and usually his or her birth and death dates. The cemetery will have a list of the people that they deal with, and the funeral home will know those people in that business. If the individual is a veteran, the VA will provide a plaque at no cost. This plaque, however, still needs to be set in a stone. Some veterans or the family may want the veteran buried in a national cemetery. Find out ahead of time if that is the desire of the person.

Contact Social Security. Depending upon when the Social Security is paid out during the month, you may have to send last month's payment back to Social Security. They can tell you if you need to do that. They also need a copy of the death certificate. Make sure to check with the funeral home about when and how they contact Social Security, if they do. It is critical that this gets done and done as soon as possible.

Contact the life insurance companies. Life insurance companies need the death certificate. They do pay out very quickly. This does imply that you know that your parent had life insurance. A year or two after my mother died, we found an old life insurance policy taken out by her parents. It was from the 1930s. It was a beautiful scrolled document, but trying to collect on that policy proved almost impossible because of its age (the company had been sold and resold) and the beneficiaries of course were all dead. Since my mother had been on Medicaid, I assume the government recovered the life insurance amount as payment toward the Medicaid costs.

Contact the pension organizations. They will also need a death certificate. The pension will either stop, or if there is a beneficiary designation on the pension, then the pension amount may be recalculated and the beneficiary begins to receive the pension (e.g., the spouse of the individual with the pension, now begins to receive the pension, but the amount may be different).

Contact credit bureaus and send them a death certificate. This eliminates any identify theft regarding the deceased person. Even in death, we have to think about identify theft. And if you are on the powers of attorney for that person, you will want to ensure that identity theft doesn't happen.

The funeral home will most likely contact the church that the person went to, but if not, you have to call the church and inform the pastor. You may want the pastor to conduct a funeral at the church or speak at the funeral home. It's whatever the individual wanted. The funeral home also may have a list of people they work with, if the family doesn't know anyone with the person's religious affiliation. Family members may want to speak at the funeral as well.

Contact the phone company, and cancel the cellular phone and landline. This also may include the cable TV and the Internet. We found cancelling the cell phone was the hardest to do. I had to give the cell company the obituary to prove that my father-in-law was dead. They may require a death certificate now.

You may have to find out the person's passwords for the Internet and cancel the Internet and any online accounts. Cancel all newspaper and magazine subscriptions and organization memberships. If the person was a veteran, the funeral home should contact the specific branch of service for a military presence at the cemetery.

All financial institutions need to be contacted (unless the spouse is still actively engaged in the finances) to cancel accounts. But wait until all the bills for the person are paid before the checking account is closed. Bills can include utility, phone, medical, and credit card bills and anything else. Depending on the time of the year, you may want to keep the bank account open until that year's taxes are paid.

The house or property has to be sold, if applicable. Or if there is a remaining spouse, you need to change the title to only contain the spouse's name. Retitle any property ownership. This saves headaches later on. Retitling is not necessary if the person is in a living revocable trust.

There are so many organizations and people to contact. Have a list ready before the person dies. It's so much easier to make the list before the death and without the time or the emotional constraints at the time of passing. Much of your previous work with the finances and the medical and daily activities will come into play here. You should have most of the contacts and most of the organizations documented.

After the Funeral

Clean out the house or remove the individual's belongings but only under the direction of the remaining spouse. We donated my dad's clothes to a homeless shelter. You may have to sell household goods as well as the house. The bills still have to be paid on the house. Grass has to be mowed, garbage taken out, the refrigerator cleaned out, and so on.

Depending on the volume of stuff in the house, you may want an estate sale. The estate sale people come into the home, arrange the items, and advertise the estate sale. They charge a percentage of the total sale as their fee. But if they are good, they will organize and display the house contents in an attractive way to sell as much as possible. The house contents have to have some level of value for it to be worth having an estate sale. Otherwise, you can always have a garage sale, sell stuff online, or give everything away.

If the spouse is alive, you need to understand what that spouse wants to do. Maybe he or she will willingly downsize. Maybe he or she wants to remain in the house. Maybe he or she wants to move to Alaska. You need to know. Sometimes it is much easier for the remaining spouse to move into an apartment or condo than live in a house that has so many memories. He or she may also want to completely redo the house and update it. Your family, I hope, will know this beforehand or have a pretty good idea what may be the next step for the surviving spouse. This decision may take time. Give it the time it needs.

If the family member was in a facility, his or her possessions need to be removed from the apartment or room where he or she resided. That needs to be done immediately. The facility will help you with that process. Obviously, the remainder of the bill for the facility will have to be paid. Some of the goods you may want to keep or donate to the facility for those people who have no family or have very little.

There will have to be thank-you cards written out to those who gave gifts or follow-up phone calls to attendees at the funeral. Many families have a favorite charity for donations given at the funeral. Those donations then need to be forwarded on to the appropriate charity.

At the beginning of the following year, you have to file the person's taxes. He or she still owes income taxes. You simply put the word "deceased" atop his or her name on the tax form. Depending on the situation, you may have to leave a bank account open until the taxes have been finalized.

Probate: Handling the Will

If you have to go through probate, the process starts immediately upon the death of the individual and can be a long and expensive process. I urge you to find a lawyer who can help you go through the probate process. In all states, there is a state bar association. Often on their website, there will be a state-specific description of the probate process. Print it out or order their brochure. It will help you navigate the process and know what to expect.

Depending on your state, there may exist a simplified probate for simple situations. Probate costs money. Probate costs *should* be paid out of the estate, not your pocket. The will is the starting point for the process, and nothing from the will can be distributed to the heirs without probate being completed. Some states have simplified the process or at least eliminated probate for very small estates (e.g. less than $50,000). The simplified process helps the executor of the will so that he or she doesn't have to appear before the probate court a lot of times. For simplified probate, usually the executor can handle everything through the Internet, faxes, and phone calls. But each state is different. You need to find out the rules for your state.

Probate is public. The executor of the estate has to appear in court multiple times (if there isn't a simplified process applicable). Creditors will be paid before heirs. The will is the first place where the probate court will look to see who the deceased person indicated as the executor. The proposed person needs to apply to be executor. The probate judge will finalize who the executor is. With no objections, it is typically the person named in the will.

Notices will be made of the estate being probated usually in the local newspaper. In some cases, in some wills, there may be an allowance for the executor as he or she carries out his or her duties. The executor will have to travel some, appear in court, take days off of work, and meet with lawyers in order to perform all duties attributable to executing a will properly.

In probate, an inventory of all assets needs to be done. Eventually this list is given to the probate judge. Appraisals need to be arranged for property inside and out. The appraisals set the value of each asset, and this goes into the probate inventory list. If there are specific collections (e.g., a stamp collection), those will need to be evaluated as well as the property and land. You can begin to see why probate takes time and costs the estate money.

I hope your process will be smooth and that your relatives will be considerate and not become greedy. Even if the estate has virtually nothing, some people believe that they deserve something. People can become very unreasonable when they think that they are getting something for nothing. We didn't experience that, and I am very grateful.

One thing to consider is the Family Medical Leave Act if you are the executor. You can use this leave to take some time handling your parents' estate. The leave can be one long continuous time, or you can take it in pieces, maybe a few days each month. You might want to contact your human resources department at your work to find out about this benefit. It may help you through this time.

After probate, the estate is divided according to the directions in the will. This is the time when property may be put up for sale. The proceeds of the sale will then pass to the heirs. The estate sale can also happen. The probate court is in place to ensure that a person's wishes regarding the disposal of his or her estate happens correctly and according to his or her directions.

If you have a living revocable trust (no probate):

When one parent dies:

Depending on what is in the trust and what is designated in the trust, assume that the remaining spouse is given all the assets. Nothing needs to be done regarding the assets. The assets immediately go under the control of the remaining spouse. Titles for property do not have to be redone because the property is already in the name of the trust. One recommendation is to have any property (land, acreage) appraised. This appraisal value will then be used for any subsequent capital gains accrued from that point onward, and that amount is used when the property is sold. Any substantial collection (art, stamps, and so on) should also be newly appraised. You need to write a letter to the probate office to declare that the person who has died has no assets. This is the same time you send in their will to the probate court. Filing the will does not start a probate process.

After this first parent dies, it would be a good time to update the asset inventory. If you want to, accounts could be closed to simplify the situation. Depending on the state within which you live and the value of the estate, there may be inheritance or death taxes applicable. Consult the attorney of record on the trust for that information.

The final taxes will have to be filed. These taxes are the same as any annual taxes for the federal and state treasuries. Just put "Deceased" above the name of the person who has died on the tax form. These taxes are done during the regular tax filing time frame the next year.

When the second parent dies:

File the will in the county where the parent died. This does not mean that a probate is required or will be started. The trust outlines what to do with the assets. The named secondary trustee(s) now takes over the assets and distributes them. The secondary trustee can close accounts, sell property, pay the bills of the estate, and eventually file the final tax returns. Consult the attorney of record for any questions, concerns, or how-tos. The trust ends at the time of the second person's death (unless the trust creates additional trusts, as in the case of a disabled child).

And yes, you need time to grieve.

There is so much to do.

Here's a condensed table of necessary items and approximate time frames when they should be accomplished. The table is a summary of what needs to be done as detailed in the previous section.

What to Do	Time Frame
Call all relatives.	Immediately
Arrange a funeral. Contact the funeral home. Contact the cemetery. Arrange for a stone. Handle the logistics with the help of the funeral home.	Immediately
Pay ongoing bills.	As needed
Close accounts that won't be needed: cable phone newspapers, subscriptions Internet	As soon as possible
Begin probate process. Find a lawyer. Find the will.	Immediately

What to Do	Time Frame
Contact Social Security, life insurance companies, and pension companies.	Immediately
Close accounts or change the name on the accounts.	As soon as possible
Retitle property if necessary.	Soon
Clean the house/condo/room. You may be using the house for a get-together after the funeral.	Soon
Sell personal property, if applicable.	After probate
Sell real estate, if applicable.	After probate
File taxes for that year. Possibly keep bank account open.	At beginning of the following year

Final Thoughts

This journey of caregiving for a parent (or loved one) is sometimes quite long and always stressful. I hope that you have found information that can help you through this. I hope you recognized that there is help, and I hope that you have learned something in these chapters that can help support you and your family. Every situation is different, but the common threads throughout this process can give you confidence as you embark on your journey.

Names of People to Call	Phone Numbers	E-mail
1.		
2.		
3.		
4.		
5.		
6.		
7.		
8.		
9.		
10.		
11.		
12.		
13.		
14.		
15.		

Names of Organizations to Call	Phone Numbers
1.	
2.	
3.	
4.	
5.	
6.	
7.	
8.	
9.	
10.	

Printed in the United States
By Bookmasters